GET CARRIED AWAY.

D1068778

So much to do. So much to see. How do you choose just one point of interest in Cleveland? Just take The Avenue to Gucci, Fendi, Bally of Switzerland, Adrienne Vittadini, The Disney Store, Lillie Rubin, Joan & David, Country Road Australia, Liz Claiborne, The Body Shop, Impostors, The Museum Company, Rand McNally, Morton's of Chicago-the Steakhouse, Fuddruckers, Sfuzzi, Hoyts Cinemas. More than 80 exclusive shops and restaurants are waiting for you on The Avenue at Tower City Center.

THE AVENUE
TOWER CITY CENTER
Open seven days a week.

in Cleveland

A guide to the city's finest

Additional copies of *In
Cleveland* may be ordered by
sending $18.95 per copy to the
address below, or by calling
1-800-234-2454, 9–5 EST,
Monday through Friday. VISA,
MC, AMEX; quantity
discounts available.

In Cleveland is published
annually by City Visitor/
Cleveland Gold, P.O. Box 612,
Hudson, Ohio 44236.
Copyright© 1991. No part of
this publication may be
reproduced or duplicated
without the express written
permission of the publisher.

Staff

Rocco A. Di Lillo
President

Donna M. Shelley
Publisher

Laura A. Alosi
Arthur P. Fisher
Advertising

Van McCulloch
Diana Safos Thusat
Mark Tisdale
Ann M. Zoller
Contributing Editors

Kathleen G. Lang
Office Manager

Kathleen Intihar
Executive Secretary

Nesnadny & Schwartz
Design

Typemasters, Inc.
Typesetting

Convention and Visitors
  Bureau of Greater Cleveland
Greater Cleveland
  Growth Association
Western Reserve Tourist Council
Memberships

Printed in the United States
of America, first edition.

Cleveland...

A pioneering spirit, forged when Cleveland

was part of the country's western frontier,

makes possible our city's great renaissance.

The nation is taking notice of the superb quality of life here in Cleveland, the heart of the North Coast of America. The city that mixes midwestern values with an east coast savvy and a west coast flair for fun.

But you don't need a surfboard to catch the wave of excitement that continues to build in downtown Cleveland and surge out into the suburbs…just a willingness to explore. And fear not. Cleveland had always been a place of hospitality. It's not surprising for us to hear a visiting New Yorker ask why we bid a friendly hello to strangers as we pass on the street. It's just the way we are.

There are other characteristics of our collective psyche that, while not as readily apparent, have held us in good stead over the years. From the beginning, this city's inhabitants have displayed exemplary tenacity, succeeding in the long run by having the ability to put obstacles aside and concentrate on the future.

A future rich with possibility, since we possess not only 90 valuable miles of freshwater coastline but also a more inestimable endowment — the courage and ingenuity of the people of northeastern Ohio. Much of Cleveland's early growth was certainly made possible by our proximity to

Cleveland's skyline continues to be enhanced as new office towers reach for the sky.

Gracious suburban living in communities such as Cleveland Heights.

by Mark Tisdale

You May Be Surprised

Cleveland is the 22nd largest city in the United States, with 536,000 residents, and is 20 square miles in area.

Lake Erie and the large, navigable Cuyahoga River, but it took men and women with vision to take advantage of it.

Beginning with the people who founded the heavy industries that flourished here during the Civil War, and continuing with the founding of large national firms such as John D. Rockefeller's Standard Oil Company, Cleveland has been fortunate in attracting the type of people who can make it happen.

This pioneering spirit combines an ability to withstand hardship with a relentless desire to succeed. And it has served us well.

The riverfront area of downtown Cleveland, known as the Flats, is an excellent example of what our ethos makes possible. This area had once thrived, experienced hard times, and was then transformed, taking on a totally new incarnation. The people of Cleveland and their will to win enabled it to happen.

Once the center for work and industry, the Flats and nearby Warehouse District are now the center for fun and diversion.

Exciting restaurants, shops, nightclubs, parks and condominiums abound, while retaining the historic essence of the area.

This type of rebirth has caused us to be known as the "Comeback City." And it has happened all over Cleveland.

Ongoing construction projects have attracted the attention of respected architectural publications such as *Progressive Architecture* and *Architectural Record*. Cleveland's skyline will continue to be enhanced as new office towers such as Society Center, Ameritrust Center, Bank One Center and Renaissance on Playhouse Square are completed, along with forthcoming (and eagerly anticipated!) projects such as the Rock-n-Roll Hall of Fame and Museum.

...aking in a fresh

...eeze off of

...ake Erie isn't

...e only way to

...joy the

...ty...but it's an

...cellent place

...start.

Also setting the pace for recent growth and change in Cleveland is the still-unfolding megadevelopment known as Tower City Center. With the Terminal Tower, downtown's venerable grand dame, as it's centerpiece, this splendidly revitalized complex is the very definition of "mixed use", providing a long-needed and vital nerve center for our city's downtown area. It houses two tall office towers, a brand new Ritz-Carlton hotel, a magnificent three-level retail center and a modernized rapid transit station.

Dedication and commitment are not reserved for our business pursuits alone; they are given to our leisure time activities as well. Take for example our ravenous appetite for professional sports . . . national sportscasters have marveled at the intensity of our fandom.

Only a city with an intrinsic resilience could weather following the Browns (they didn't call them the Kardiac Kids in the early 80's for nothing) and heaven knows, our beloved Indians. And there's always plenty of passion left for the NBA Cavs and the MSL Crunch.

In addition to having four professional sports teams, Cleveland also has cultural amenities galore, including a world class ballet company and, of course, the world renowned Cleveland Orchestra.

The list of positive attributes is lengthy indeed. Annual cost of living indexes have consistently proven Cleveland to be one of our country's most affordable major metropolitan areas. And the sheer number and quality of our golf courses alone have attracted many people here. If you prefer an

afternoon of chukkers, the nearby polo grounds in the beautiful Chagrin Valley can accommodate you.

The Cleveland Museum of Art is ranked as one of the top five museums in the country. And if you wished to have the best cardiologists in the world attend to you, where would you go? Ask Jordan's King Hussein or the Emir of Bahrain, they are just two of the many world leaders who entrust their care to the Cleveland Clinic.

Cleveland is a city that has so much history, character and cultural opportunity . . . experience and enjoy. Go out and explore the city and discover for yourself why it is perhaps the best kept secret in the nation. Only then will you begin to understand why it has earned its respect — for having not only the guts to be a survivor, but the resilience and determination to overcome all obstacles and become a winner.

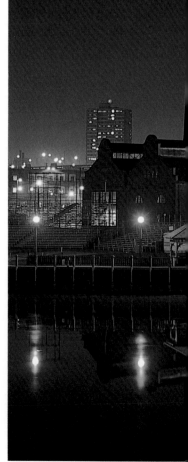

The Port of Cleveland (the 3rd largest overseas general cargo port on the Great Lakes) serves more than 50 countries, shipping cargo to, and receiving from, 120 ports around the world.

d-class retail complex.

Could Cleveland be the best kept secret in the land? Yes, but word is getting out.

The Nautica Entertainment Complex, on the west bank of Cleveland's Flats.

From downtown to the suburbs, Cleveland

is a sophisticated retail center.

Shops & Indulgences

The Cleveland Play House, founded in 1915, is the country's oldest regional theatre.

The Arcade

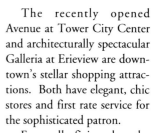

by Diana Safos Thusat

The recently opened Avenue at Tower City Center and architecturally spectacular Galleria at Erieview are downtown's stellar shopping attractions. Both have elegant, chic stores and first rate service for the sophisticated patron.

For mall aficionados, the suburban selection and caliber is top-notch. From Beachwood's famous Beachwood Place mall to Rocky River's intimate Beachcliff Market Square there are numerous shopping facilities to suit individual tastes and temperaments.

If urban shopping is preferred, then take a stroll down Euclid Avenue from Public Square to E. 12th Street. The May Company and Higbee's, two of Cleveland's oldest and finest department stores, can be found there along with contemporary boutiques and specialty shops. The Arcade, a must-see treasured landmark, (stretching between Euclid and Superior avenues at E. 6th Street) houses eateries and exclusive shops.

In addition to the malls and downtown commercial district, Cleveland has several unique shopping locales. A trip to Chagrin Falls, a quaint eastern suburb, is a delightful excursion; the gazebo on the town square and natural waterfall add to its splendor. Coventry Road in Cleveland Heights, between Mayfield Road and Euclid Heights Boulevard, is another worthwhile trek. Ethnically and economically diverse, it's a stone's-throw away from University Circle. And Shaker Square, on Cleveland's east side, is an eclectic mix of fascinating shops.

15

Kilgore Trout, at the Eton Collection

KILGORE TROUT

MEN'S AND WOMEN'S APPAREL   ETON COLLECTION   28601 CHAGRIN BLVD.   TEL (216) 831 0488

**The Avenue at
Tower City Center**
Downtown on
Public Square.

Cleveland's newest shopping center, The Avenue, is home to the most exclusive shops in the city. Symbolizing the area's resurgence, it represents the "new Cleveland" — exciting, upscale and growing. And it's bringing people downtown again by providing the setting for elaborate special events, as well as the finest in shopping and dining. Two of its stores, Liz Claiborne and the Disney Store, lead their respective chains in American sales. The Avenue's magnificent art deco design is the result of a recent, massive restoration project which returned it to its original, 1920s splendor. Its central downtown location is easily accessible by bus and rapid transit train, and connected underground parking spaces are plentiful. Valet parking is also available.

Open Mon.-Fri. 10 am
to 9 pm; Saturday 10
am to 6 pm.; Sunday
12 pm to 6 pm.

771-0049
771-0033

Beachcliff Market Square
19300 Detroit Road,
Rocky River.

This award winning re-adaptation and expansion of a 1930s movie theatre is in the genre of Ghirardelli Square in San Francisco and Faneuil Hall Marketplace in Boston. It is Cleveland's specialty shopping source for fine clothing and jewelry, personal services ranging from hair styling to skin care, and incomparable giftware and home furnishings. As you consider your purchases, sample the Euro-American cuisine of Heck's Cafe or the Szechuan sauces of Pearl of the Orient, two of Cleveland's consistently top rated restaurants. Explore the offerings of 26 shops with the personal assistance of shopkeepers who have searched the market places of the world for uncommon excellence. Beachcliff Market Square is still a showplace.

Open Tues.-Fri. 10 am
to 9 pm; Mon. & Sat.
10 am to 5:30 pm;
Sundays during the
holiday season 12 pm
to 5 pm.

333-5074

The Avenue at Tower City Center   Gucci, on the Avenue at Tower City Center

IF YOU'RE

TOO BUSY

TO STOP

AND SMELL

THE FLOWERS,

JUST PICK UP

THE PHONE.

18

Gluchov Diamonds & Gems

Brunswick & Son Florist

9650 Carnegie Avenue

Cleveland, Ohio 44106

216/421-4800

Golland Shoes

Beachwood Place

On the east side;
26300 Cedar Road,
Beachwood.

More than just a mall, Beachwood Place is a social gathering place for the community. Beachwood Place features over 100 fine shops, services and restaurants. Among their offerings are The Coach Store, Country Road Australia, Mondi, Rodier, Laura Ashley, Mother and Child, Ann Taylor and Lillie Rubin.

Greater Cleveland's first upscale mall, it continues to rely on exclusive shops which carry the top names in fashion design. Saks Fifth Avenue launched its first, and only, Cleveland store at Beachwood Place and its success encouraged other quality retailers to locate here.

Open Mon.- Sat. 10
am to 9 pm; Sunday
12 pm to 5 pm.

464-9460

Benetton

While famous for its brightly colored sweaters and youth apparel, Benetton also offers a wide range of professional and leisure clothing for both men and women. Classic, traditional pieces have been updated with colorful fabric and European styling. High quality suits, skirts, slacks, topcoats, jackets, shorts, shoes, dresses and accessories are available in wool, cotton and other natural materials. The emphasis on quality, detailing and coordinating pieces makes Benetton's stand-out clothing a worldwide sensation.

Open Mon.-Sat. 10
am to 9 pm; Sunday
12 pm to 5 pm (Tower
City). Hours for other
stores vary. Please call
for further information.

The Avenue 696-3555
Beachwood 831-8331
Chagrin Falls 247-6349
Hudson 656-3355
Great Northern 779-4404

Jewels By IMG

Fendi, on The Avenue at Tower City Center

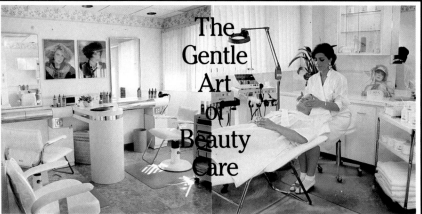

Laurèl (left) and Adam Ross (right), both at The Galleria at Erieview.

Brunswick and Son Florist
9650 Carnegie Avenue, across from the Cleveland Clinic, in University Circle.

Cleveland's premier florist for more than 60 years, Brunswick and Son always attends to the smallest detail and provides quality floral designs, ranging from traditional to contemporary. Expertise in planning arrangements appropriate for extravagant galas, intimate parties, special occasions and executive gifts. Only the freshest flowers, imported daily from around the world, are used. What makes Brunswick and Son unique is its exciting selection of hard to find tropicals, exotic and Dutch garden varieties, as well as seasonal domestics. Delivery is limited to Cuyahoga County and is guaranteed same day on orders received before 11 am. Out of town delivery is available through all major wire services.

Open Mon.-Sat. 8:30 am to 5:30 pm.   AE, MC,Visa and Discover accepted.

421-4800

The Galleria at Erieview

21

Christopher's Clothiers
Downtown,
1801 E. 9th Street.

Founded in 1974, Christopher's has earned the reputation as one of Cleveland's leading men's clothiers. Specializing in updated-traditional stylings, Christopher's offers a wide variety of suits, sportscoats, slacks, shirts, ties, outerwear and sportswear, as well as all the accessories necessary to complete your wardrobe. From classic traditional to cutting edge double-breasted models, Christopher's has the suits that fit your style. Value pricing combined with outstanding service and tailoring is why Christopher's is the choice of the Cleveland businessman.

Open Mon.– Fri. 9:30
am to 6 pm; Saturday
10 am to 5 pm. Closed
Sunday.
AE, MC, and Visa
accepted.

621-6333

The Professional Woman

Everyone wants to think they have something no one else has . . .
from someone extra special . . . and it'll last forever . . .
I give them that. I know it.

Jm. Greenberg

Fena's Skin Care Clinic
21625 Chagrin Blvd.,
Beachwood.

If you enjoy being pampered, you will enjoy a day at Fena's. Catering only to women, this full service salon offers total body care by European trained aestheticians. The products used contain only natural ingredients and all treatments are administered on an individual basis in private rooms. A wide variety of deep cleansing facials, body and skin treatments, body waxing, hair care, and smile enhancement services (provided by Dr. H.N. Silverman) are available.

Changing rooms, a lunchroom, Jacuzzi and shower are located on the premises for each customer's complete comfort.

Open Mon.-Sat. 9 am to 6 pm; Thursdays 9 am to 9 pm. By appointment only.

561-3362

photo-illustration by Benjamin Margalit

"NATIONAL AWARD-WINNING JEWELRY DESIGNER"

ORIGINAL DESIGNED JEWELRY
14K & 18K GOLD & PLATINUM
ALL WORK DONE ON PREMISES

Jewels By

© 1990 IMG

5470 Mayfield Road • Lyndhurst, Ohio 44124
Local: (216) 461-9550
National: (800) 321-6317
FAX: (216) 461-0087

TRANSPORTATION PROVIDED FROM YOUR HOTEL TO OUR SHOWROOM

Fendi
Downtown, on
The Avenue
at Tower City Center.

Clevelanders no longer need to go to New York or Rome for Fendi fashions. Instead, they can shop right downtown at Fendi's second largest United States store.

The full Fendi collection offers exquisite selections for business, leisure and formal affairs. The high fashion, ready-to-wear line is designed by Karl Lagerfeld and made with only the finest natural fabrics. Leather goods are also a mainstay of Fendi, with handbags, coats, jackets, shoes, belts and other items being featured. The Fendi furs are breathtaking, and a handsome array of jewelry and watches is available as well.

Open Mon.-Fri. 10 am to 9 pm; Saturday 10 am to 6 pm; Sunday 12 pm to 6 pm.

AE, MC and Visa accepted.

696-6264

23

United Colors of Benetton

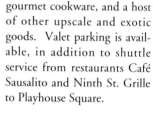

The Forgotten Woman

Paris, fine fragrances, records, books, luggage, toys, candy, gourmet cookware, and a host of other upscale and exotic goods. Valet parking is available, in addition to shuttle service from restaurants Café Sausalito and Ninth St. Grille to Playhouse Square.

Open Mon.-Sat. 10 am to 8 pm; Sundays and holidays 11 am to 6 pm.

621-9999

The Forgotten Woman
The Galleria at Erieview,
E. 9th Street at St. Clair
Avenue.

Designer clothes for the plus size woman never looked so good. The Forgotten Woman's extensive collection of quality apparel ranges from the elegant to the unusual. Only the best fashion lines, such as Givenchy, Evan Picone, Harvé Bernard, Judith Ann, and Pantages grace the premises. Outfits appropriate for any occasion can be coordinated by the attentive, knowledgeable staff. Sportswear, suiting, evening wear, coats, swimwear, sleepwear, and lingerie are available in sizes 14 to 24; shoes and boots are available in wide and extra-wide sizes from 7 to 12.

Open Mon.-Sat. 10 am to 6 pm; Sundays and holidays noon to 5 pm.

621-8880

The Galleria at Erieview
Downtown,
E. 9th Street at
St. Clair Avenue.

For convenience, accessibility, and a pleasant environment nothing beats a leisurely shopping excursion to The Galleria at Erieview. A ten minute walk from both Public Square and the downtown lakeshore, this three-year-old structure follows the original design of world-famous architect I.M. Pei. Natural light is filtered through a glass arched roof onto marble floors and sixty-foot columns. Discriminating patrons can find designer fashions, leather wear, sports shoes, travel and safari clothing, jewelry from

Gluchov Diamonds & Gems
La Place mall
2101 Richmond Rd.,
Beachwood (at Cedar and Richmond roads).

From the exquisite antique jewelry to the elegantly styled display cases, tradition and grace permeate this establishment. Proprietor Marc Gluchov specializes in diamonds, antique and estate jewelry, precious gems, and fine watches. If you are looking for select, one of a kind pieces, then this old-line jeweler is for you. The repair service is also first class; vintage items that others do not or cannot mend are lovingly restored.

Open Mon.-Sat. 10 am to 5:30 pm; Thurs. 10 am to 8 pm. Additional hours by appointment.

464-6424

Beachcliff Market Square

Golland Shoes For Men
Downtown on The
Avenue at Tower City
Center; and east at
Beachwood Place mall.

Founded in 1950, this family-owned business stocks only the finest in high fashion, businessmen's, and casual shoes. Footwear lines such as Allen Edmonds, Bally, Cole-Haan, Clark's of England, R. Martegani, Lorenzo Banfi, Bostonian, Rockport, Timberland, Sebago, Sperry, Marco Luigi, and Church's Famous English Shoes are displayed in an atmosphere reminiscent of a well-bred gentleman's dressing room. Fine quality hosiery, leather accessories, Bally sportswear and shoe maintenance products are also available. The professional, knowledgeable sales staff provides excel-lent service. The store offers free delivery to customers anywhere in the United States.

Store hours Mon.-Fri. 10 am to 9 pm. Sat. 10 am to 6 pm. Sunday (at Tower City) 12 pm to 6 pm. (at Beachwood Place) 12 pm to 5 pm.

AE, MC, Visa, Diners Club and Carte Blanche accepted.

623-1750 Downtown
464-6388 Beachwood

26

Beachcliff Market Square

Jewels By IMG
5470 Mayfield Rd.,
Lyndhurst.

This premier jewelry salon is intensively customer oriented, offering personal consultations in private sitting rooms. Owner Isadore M. Greenberg is nationally known for his unique, award-winning designs and gracious treatment. Celebrities such as Stephanie Powers, Liberace and Sammy Davis, Jr. have come to IMG for exclusive jewelry. All pieces are custom-made on the premises by craftsmen using the finest precious stones and metals. Specialty items include rings for the arthritic, gold braille watches, gold fingernails and eyelashes.

Showroom hours Mon.– Fri. 9:30 am to 5:30 pm; Sat. 9 am to 5 pm; Tues. evening only by appointment; special designs by appointment. Transportation provided to and from hotels.

461-9550

Shopping 27

Christopher's Clothiers

28

Kilgore Trout

On the east side at the
Eton Collection,
28601 Chagrin Blvd.

For 14 years, Clevelanders have known that Kilgore Trout is the place for clothing with a smashing sense of taste and style. Each customer receives the personal service to find just the piece or ensemble they are looking for. Suits, separates, sportswear, tailored clothing and accessories are available for both men and women, while formal-wear and shoes are available for men only. A wide range of top designer lines such as Ermenegildo Zegna, Giorgio Armani, Krizia Uomo, Byblos, Umberto Ginochietti and Iceberg are carried by Kilgore Trout, in addition to its own exclusive Italian-made line,

Moda Firenza. Custom tailoring for men and free alterations for both men and women are also available.

Open Mon. – Sat 10 am to 6 pm; Thursday 10 am to 9 pm.

AE, MC and Visa accepted.

831-0488

The Professional Woman

Beachwood Place; Downtown 1801 E. 9th St.; Great Northern Mall.

This Ohio chain of women's clothing stores reflects everything that the name implies. With the largest collection of tailored suits and packaged shirts in the area, these shops are essential for women who must appear well-groomed and traditional for their careers. The stores feature the Gail Gordon Collection, an exclusive line evoking Calvin Klein and Ralph Lauren styling. They are also the only Ohio retailer of Burberry's entire clothing collection. Seminars and light luncheons with informal fashion shows take place both in-store and off-site at corporate offices. A frequent shopper program is available as well as alterations. Clothes range in size from 2 to 20, petites from 2 to 16.

Beachwood Place Mall & Great Northern Mall: Mon.-Sat. 10 am to 9 pm; Sun. 12 pm to 5 pm. Downtown: Mon.-Fri. 9 am to 6 pm; Sat. 10 am to 5 pm; closed Sun.

All major credit cards accepted.

464-3100 Beachwood
781-3373 Downtown
779-0666 Gr. Northern

Cactus, at The Galleria at Erieview

BEACHWOOD PLACE

Shopping like no other place.

Saks Fifth Avenue, Higbee's and 100 fine shops, restaurants and services. Cedar and Richmond Roads. One quarter mile west of I-271.
Open 10 A.M. to 9 P.M. Monday through Saturday; Sunday Noon to 5 P.M. For more information, 216-464-9460.

Merchandise provided by Bailey, Banks & Biddle, Cache, Deering Gallery, and FootPrint.

the Arts

Cleveland's artistic community flourishes in one

of the country's most conducive environments for creative expression.

Wade Oval, at University Circle

Performing & Visual Arts

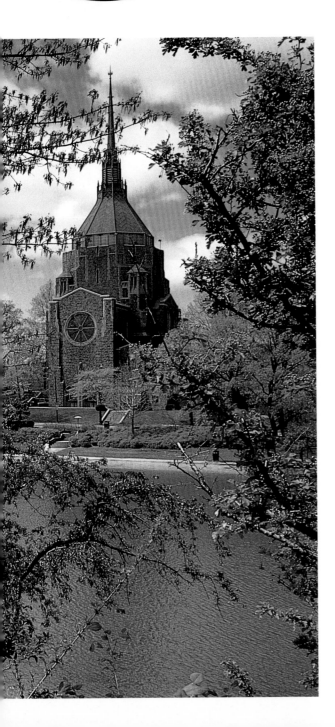

by Diana Safos Thusat

Aesthetes of the world will be happy to find Greater Cleveland's cultural life in a healthy, vigorous condition. Both the performing and visual arts are well represented and are thriving under public and corporate support and appreciation. Each major performing art is professionally represented by internationally renowned companies, and the visual arts are promoted by gallery owners and museum directors committed to artistic excellence.

One epicenter for Cleveland's cultural activity is University Circle. The Circle is home to the Cleveland Orchestra and five outstanding museums, including The Cleveland Museum of Art. It is also home to many art galleries, which abound in Greater Cleveland. Other areas with dense concentrations of art galleries include Little Italy, Shaker Square and downtown's Warehouse District.

For ballet and live theatre, the place to be is Playhouse Square. The 7,000 seats among three theatres (the Ohio, Palace and State), make this conglomerate the country's third largest performing arts center. Each theatre presents plays and musicals performed by top entertainers and original Broadway casts. Two other premier complexes are The Cleveland Play House and Karamu House.

34

75th Anniversaries

Cleveland's long-standing tradition of cultural excellence is highlighted this year with three 75th anniversaries. Celebrating are The Cleveland Museum of Art, The Cleveland Play House, and Karamu House.

The Museum's special exhibitions are on display from June 1991 to September 1992. *Notable Acquisitions* exhibits the most significant additions to the Museum's collection during the past two years (all being shown for the first time), and *Celebration!* chronicles the Museum's development.

The Cleveland Play House continues its commitment to presenting new American plays and old classics as it drops the curtain on its 75th season in June. Karamu House maintains its proud tradition of multi-cultural theatre as it continues its 75th anniversary season through June.

Great Performances

What a glorious town this is for dazzling entertainment ranging from Broadway productions to Cleveland's own world renowned orchestra. Whether it is classical, contemporary or avant-garde, Cleveland offers the best in music, theatre and dance.

One of the city's greatest treasures is **The Cleveland Orchestra.** Established in 1918, it is respected internationally as being one of the world's finest orchestras. Its reputation for excellence grew under the direction of George Szell, who was the conductor from 1946 to 1970. Szell embarked on several extensive foreign tours with the orchestra, as well as expanding its commercial recording repertoire.

Currently, The Cleveland Orchestra is under the direction of conductor Christoph von Dohnányi, whose praises have been sung by many music critics such as Andrew Porter of The New Yorker, "Wisdom, judgement, strength of personality, and integrity of feeling mark his work. Uncommon technical accomplishment also plays its part: under Dohnányi's leadership, the Cleveland is again what it was under Szell —one of the world's great orchestras."

The Cleveland Orchestra performs at **Severance Hall** in University Circle from September through May. During the summer months, the orchestra plays in the open-air amphitheater at Blossom Music Center, which is centrally located between Cleveland and Akron.

Head west of University Circle toward downtown Cleveland, to find the **Playhouse Square Center.** This group of three renovated theatres, the Ohio, Palace and State, is the third largest entertainment complex in North America, and consistently draws first-rate performers.

Playhouse Square Foundation, the organization that manages the theatres, has become a nationally recognized incubator of new American musical productions as well as a successful producer.

The world
renowned
Cleveland
Orchestra
performs locally
at Severance
Hall.

To date the company has produced and presented the acclaimed *Gospel at Colonus* on Broadway after initiating the production at the State Theatre, and co-produced *Big River* and *Pump Boys & Dinettes* for national tour.

The Playhouse Square Foundation has presented hundreds of pop entertainers, comedians, touring musicals and international attractions including: the Rat Pack with Frank Sinatra and Sammy Davis, Jr.; the Legends of Comedy with Milton Berle, Danny Thomas and Sid Ceasar; the Manhattan Transfer; *Phantom of the Opera; Cats;* and *Les Miserables.*

The theatres themselves are worth visiting just to enjoy their magnificent architecture and loving restorations. Singer Linda Ronstadt was so taken with the Palace that she asked to see the other theatres after the crowds left. The three theatres were built in the 1920s as vaudeville houses and are listed on the National Register of Historic Places. The renovation of the theatres, at a cost of $37.7 million, has distinguished Playhouse Square Center as the largest theatre restoration project in the world.

Playhouse Square also hosts several resident companies including the Cleveland Ballet, Great Lakes Theater Festival and Cleveland Opera.

Founded by Dennis Nahat and Ian Horvath, former American Ballet Theater dancers, the **Cleveland Ballet** is the fifth largest ballet company in the nation. Known in California as San Jose Cleveland Ballet, the company is recognized for performances in the grand theatrical style. Its ever-widening repertoire includes choreography by Bournonville, Flindt, Limon, Lichine, Balanchine, and deMille. The Cleveland Ballet performs matinees and evenings at the State Theatre; this years schedule includes *All American Dance, Romeo and Juliet,* and *Coppelia.*

The **Great Lakes Theater Festival,** founded by Arthur Lithgow, will celebrate its 30th anniversary in July 1992. The Festival presents classics of all theatrical eras — from the poetry of Shakespeare to the wit of Shaw, from the emotion of Chekov and Ibsen to the melodies of Broadway's golden age. Utilizing the beautifully appointed Ohio Theatre as its home, it continues to attract the country's finest talents. (Tom Hanks performed with the company in the late 1970s.)

The **Cleveland Opera** celebrates its 15th anniversary this year. Formed as the city's resident opera company, it first sought to develop a strong audience base by performing most of its works in English. Also appealing to the masses is its repertoire, which will please both neophytes and opera aficionados. Classics such as Faust and Aida have been performed as well as the operettas *Naughty Marietta* and *Kiss Me, Kate.*

Another long-standing

The Cleveland Museum of Art

member of Cleveland's performing arts community is **The Cleveland Play House.** Founded in 1915, it is the country's oldest regional (professional, non-profit) theatre. The Play House's three theatres, the Bolton, Brooks and Drury, are housed in one complex which was designed by internationally acclaimed architect Philip Johnson. It stretches between Euclid and Carnegie avenues at East 86th Street.

The Cleveland Play House is committed to artistic achievement and has nurtured prominent actors such as Joel Grey, Ray Walston, Alan Alda, Margaret Hamilton and Dom DeLuise. Today, the theatre continues to stage first-rate productions with talented entertainers such as Marlo Thomas, Daniel J. Travanti, Bill Cobbs, Tammy Grimes and Joe Mascolo. Currently under the artistic direction of Josephine R. Abady, the Play House continues to attract national recognition for its commitment to producing new American plays.

The Cleveland Metroparks System, containing 19,000 acres of land, is the 2nd largest municipal park system in the United States.

Walk down the street to East 89th and Quincy Avenue and to find another Cleveland treasure, **Karamu House.** Founded in 1915 by white social workers Rowena and Russell Jelliffe, the theatre was committed to interracial artistic productions at a time when segregation was the norm. Karamu, which is Swahili for "a place of joyful meeting," continues to serve the Black community by promoting new artistic endeavors.

Smaller local theatres worth visiting include the Lakewood Little Theatre/Beck Center, Cleveland Public Theatre, Dobama Theatre, and **Cain Park.** Built into the contours of a wooded ravine, Cain Park's magnificent 4,000 seat, open-air amphitheater presents an outstanding variety of community-oriented programs. This summer theatre is run by the City of Cleveland Heights. For more than half a century, the live performances and visual arts displays beneath the stars have enriched the lives of Greater Clevelanders.

Museums

Cleveland's rich cultural heritage is nowhere more visible than through its collection of acclaimed museums. No other city in the world offers such a dense concentration of cultural institutions as Cleveland's **University Circle** area. A proud legacy of monetary and land bequests from area philanthropists stands behind the five major museums:

The Cleveland Museum of Art, celebrating its 75th anniversary this year, opened its doors to the public on June 6, 1916. The Museum is one of the finest in the country and its prestigious collections are world famous. More than 48,000 works of art representing a wide range of cultures and periods are permanently on display.

Noted for its impressive collection of Asian and Medieval European artwork, The Cleveland Museum of Art also boasts an outstanding array of Egyptian, Greek, Roman, African, and pre-Columbian art.

Each year several traveling shows move through the special exhibition galleries, but the museum's own May Show remains one of the most popular. Begun in 1919 as the Annual Exhibition of Cleveland Artists & Craftsmen, the May Show (held each spring, though not necessarily in the month of

39

The Cleveland Museum of Natural History

May) displays the work of Northeast Ohio's most talented artists.

The Cleveland Museum of Art, a private and non-profit institution, continues its deep commitment to the public by maintaining a generous free admission policy. Another institution devoted to the public is **The Cleveland Museum of Natural History**. Founded in 1920 by local attorney Harold Clark, the Museum's purpose was, and is, to enable people to understand and appreciate our physical environment. It is the largest museum in Ohio dedicated specifically to natural history, conservation and environmental education.

Located on the edge of Wade Oval, across the street from the Art Museum, the Cleveland Museum of Natural History contains four large display galleries, a living-animal section, a planetarium, an observatory, a research library, an auditorium and temporary exhibit galleries.

The Museum's most popular exhibitions are reconstructed prehistoric animals, which especially thrill and delight children. Dinosaurs, a giant elk, a saber-toothed cat and an American mastodon stand as reminders of the Ice Age. Special exhibits high-

lighting an array of prehistoric creatures always attract record crowds.

Permanently on display in the Hall of Earth Sciences are precious gemstones, fluorescent minerals and intricate crystals from around the world. In addition to its fabulous exhibits, The Cleveland Museum of Natural History offers lectures, films, field trips and classes for the entire family.

Another museum complex on the edge of Wade Oval is **The Western Reserve Historical Society**, which is comprised of the History Museum, History Library, and Crawford Auto-Aviation Museum. Founded in 1867, the Historical Society is the oldest existing cultural institution in Cleveland. Open year-round, it is the largest privately supported regional historical collection in the country. Among its original benefactors were John D. Rockefeller, Charles Baldwin and Charles Whittlesey.

The History Museum is housed in two magnificent early-20th century mansions. Both homes are Italian Renaissance in style and feature exquisite architectural detailing, woodwork, iron-work and large formal gardens. Extensive collections of American furniture and decorative arts are displayed in more than 20 period rooms which highlight the finest in American and European furnishings from the mid-18th century to the 1920s. Glass, silver, ceramics, costumes, paintings and domestic implements are located throughout the Museum and in special exhibition galleries and displays.

The Crawford Auto-Aviation Museum contains more than 150 antique, vintage and classic automobiles, motorcycles and rare aircraft. It was opened in 1965 after receiving a collection of historical automobiles and aircraft from TRW, Inc.

Included in the museum's collection is the oldest closed automobile known to exist in North America, an 1895 Panhard et Levassor. A more recent addition is a 1981 Aston Martin Lagonda. These cars and the entire collection represent the technological and stylistic advancement of the automobile.

While not properly a museum, **The Garden Center of Greater Cleveland**, which also sits on the edge of Wade Oval, is another worthwhile stop. It is the oldest civic garden center in the United States and contains the largest garden center library in the country. Founded in 1930, The Garden Center was "to offer a place where all people may come for information on landscape problems, where people may study books and data on gardens, flowers, plant life, and landscape work, where monthly exhibits may illustrate and instruct in the art of gardening."

In fulfilling its mission to educate the public about flora, The Garden Center conducts tours, lectures, classes, workshops, and clinics for gardeners, home owners, and specialists.

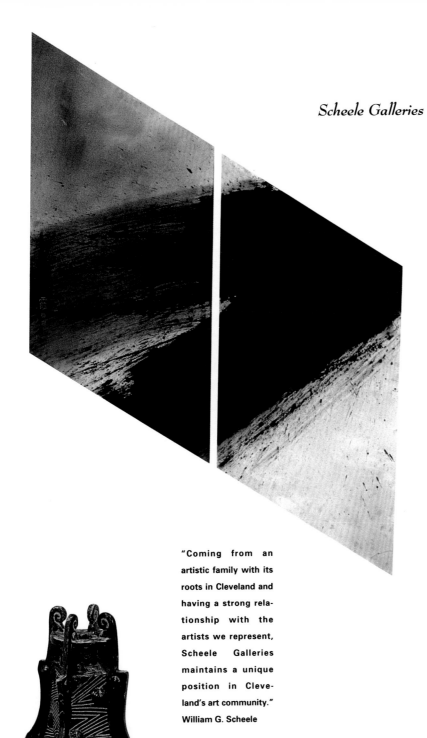

Scheele Galleries

"Coming from an artistic family with its roots in Cleveland and having a strong relationship with the artists we represent, Scheele Galleries maintains a unique position in Cleveland's art community."
William G. Scheele

Scheele Galleries Inc.
The Rockefeller Bldg.
3095 Mayfield Road,
in Cleveland Heights

(216) 321-0600

Scheele Galleries provides Cleveland with a wide variety of quality historic and contemporary artwork including painting, prints, sculpture, glass, ceramics and wearable art. And while the Gallery's strength lies in regional artists, nationally and internationally recognized artists are also represented.

Some of the historic painters and printmakers include John James Audubon, Charles Burchfield, Stanley W. Hayter, Rockwell Kent, Pablo Picasso, John Sloan and Victor Vasarely. Gallery Director William G. Scheele is considered to be the authority on the regional Cleveland School artists, and represents the estates of Frank Wilcox, Paul Travis and William Grauer.

Another forte is the number of renowned natural history artists represented. Scheele Galleries is fortunate to manage the estate of Charles R. Knight (1874-1953, NYC) who was the first artist to accurately portray prehistoric animals. Several contemporary artists who were influenced by Knight are also represented, such as William E. Scheele, Mark Hallett, William Stout and David Rankin.

Comtemporary artists exhibiting at the gallery include Alexander Aitken, Will Barnet, Clarence Carter, Kenneth Marcus Hugh, Kasumi, Joseph O'Sickey, Syd Solomon, Charles Herndon, David Hostetler, William McVey, Gary Spinosa, Auke Zandstra, Donna Webb, Rene Fuller, Margaret Netherton and Dorothy Widen.

Scheele Galleries offers a variety of arts related services including appraisals, an artwork leasing program, software packages for collectors, corporate and private art consultation, exhibition curating, restoration and custom framing.

"We carry museum quality art, at prices people can afford."
Tom and Linda Riley

Riley Hawk Galleries
2026 Murray Hill Road
Little Italy/University
Circle area

(216) 421-1445

As one of the top five glass art galleries in the United States, Riley Hawk is riding the crest of a new wave in glass art.

Because the United States leads the world in the refinement and creation of glass art, that places the gallery in the vanguard internationally. In turn, glass art itself leads the worldwide three-dimensional art movement.

This explosion in three-dimensional glass art began 30 years ago in Toledo, Ohio with Harvey Littleton, who is considered the father of the modern glass art surge. Littleton's work, as well as that of his proteges and other internationally revered glass artists, can be seen at Riley Hawk. The emphasis of the gallery is on quality, contemporary art by artists whose pieces have been purchased by the Louvre, the Metropolitan Museum of Art and other internationally acclaimed museums.

"We carry museum quality art at prices people can afford," says owner Tom Riley. "The quality is very high, the same as in New York City, and people know that they can buy from us with confidence."

What makes glass art especially exciting today is the maturity of the field; according to Riley "The materials are much more sophisticated today than they were 30 years ago." Riley Hawk emphasizes in-depth works of internationally renowned glass artists such as Harvey Littleton, Dale Chihuly, Christopher Ries, Jon Kuhn, Paul Stankard, Damian Priour, William Morris, Steve Weinberg, William Carlson, Dan Dailey and Paul Manners.

Riley's personal commitment to the artists and the gallery comes from a deep appreciation of glass art and a commitment to the aesthetic quality of life in greater Cleveland. His special pride in thecity and its cultural milieu is reflected in Riley Hawk Galleries.

A spectacular work by glass artist Dale Chihuly.

Brenda Kroos Gallery

Building on primary themes of quality and diversity, Brenda Kroos Gallery showcases some of today's finest contemporary (both abstract and realistic) art in all mediums, including paintings, sculpture and limited edition prints. Focusing on nationally and internationally acclaimed artists, Cleveland native Brenda Kroos brings the cutting edge to our city.

Kroos' philosophy of showing innovative, dynamic works translates into a fresh approach in presenting art.

The emphasis is on aesthetic enrichment and "education through exposure" rather than just sales. Patrons are encouraged to browse as they would in a museum. And the space itself invites leisurely reflection; encompassing 1,800 square feet with just the gallery and 5,000 square feet in total, this is one of Cleveland's largest galleries, and each piece is given a spacious and dramatic presentation.

In addition to fine art, limited editions, reproductions and posters, the gallery offers a wide range of consulting services for corporations, small businesses, institutions and private residences. "Adding art to a person's physical and mental environment has taken on an importance which requires both time and aesthetic judgement," says Kroos, "with our resources and expertise, we can assist in this process."

We are trying to contribute to the cultural life of the city, and broaden Clevelanders' scope of art awareness," says Kroos, **"by focusing on art from outside of the area."**

Downtown, the
Warehouse District
1360 West Ninth
Street

(216) 621-1164

Brenda Kroos Gallery

A visitor who ventures a few blocks west of University Circle can find the **Cleveland Health Education Museum** on Euclid Avenue. Founded in 1936 to help educate the public on health related matters, this is the oldest permanent health museum in the country.

The Museum promotes well-being in all areas of life. Its goal is to educate the individual as well as the health care professional. It generated the nation's first sex education classes for elementary and secondary school children, and was a pioneer in drug education. The Museum developed programs for the elderly and the disabled.

The Cleveland Health Education Museum galleries were designed for dramatic visual appeal, while retaining scholarly integrity. "See, hear and touch" is the rule in this hands-on environment. The challenge for the museum is to translate an idea into an educational participatory display.

Another user-friendly museum in the area is the **Cleveland Children's Museum.** Located in University Circle on Euclid Avenue, this Museum was opened in 1986 for children between the ages 3-12. The Museum is a multi-sensory, creative learning environment with three room-sized exhibits which parents and kids can enjoy through hands-on experience and a range of learning opportunities. Exhibits incorporate more than 100 activities through manipulating objects, role playing and fantasy, and social interaction.

Smaller but equally intriguing area museums outside of University Circle include the African-American Museum, Cleveland Police Historical Society Museum, Great Lakes Historical Society,

and Harriet Tubman Museum & Cultural Association.

Galleries

The opportunity for artists to create and display their works in Cleveland has never been better. With both traditional spaces and a variety of non-traditional exhibition areas, all forms and styles of art can find a niche in the city. Artists are attracted here by the magnetism of a strongly supportive public.

One especially strong artistic enclave is Cleveland's University Circle and its adjacent neighborhood, Little Italy. Artists are able to live, work and exhibit their creations in this culturally distinct district. The fountainhead for much of this area's art is the **Cleveland Institute of Art.** The Institute takes pride in its students' works, which are presented for public viewing during the school's periodic showings. The Reinberger Galleries, with 5,000 sq. ft., is the second largest gallery in Cleveland.

Another institutional gallery in the area is Case Western Reserve University's **Mather Gallery.** Eight shows are organized each year from September through May. The gallery's special curatorial interests include contemporary sculpture, Black Art, and performing art. Items can be purchased directly through the gallery; three weeks after a show closes buyers are directed to the individual artists.

Up the hill in the quaint Little Italy neighborhood, several distinct art galleries line Murray Hill Road. **Avante Gallery,** which is operated by ceramic artist Tom Huck, displays only three-dimensional art. With a healthy balance between regional and national artists, the gallery offers contemporary, expressionistic ceramic, glass and sculpted pieces. The gallery

promotes progressive work and art that is created by using obscure media.

Fiori Studio Gallery, operated by handmade paper artists David Batz and Robert Jursinski, carries a broad range of contemporary regional and national artwork. From paintings and crafts to photographs, this combined shop and gallery values all forms of artistic expression. In addition to its six shows per year, the gallery participates in the Murray Hill Art Walks, held the first weeks of December and June of each year.

The Murray Hill Market, currently celebrating its tenth year in operation, is one of the oldest galleries on the street. The gallery specializes in fine contemporary crafts by Cleveland and American artists The art is created from glass, wood, pewter, ceramics and textiles—and most of it is functional. Represented are more than 400 national artists who create glass and ceramic sculptures, jewelry, ornaments, toys, vases, cutting boards, scarves, wooden musical instruments, jewel boxes, handmade greeting cards and other crafts.

Riley Hawk Galleries represents prominent national and international glass artists such as Dale Chihuly, Harvey Littleton, William Morris, Steve Weinberg and William Carlson. Jewelry, sculptures, vases and paper weights are displayed during the gallery's six annual shows. One-person shows scheduled for this year include the following artists: Sally Rogers, John Kuhn, William Morris, and optical glass sculptor Christopher Ries.

William Busta Gallery, also located on Murray Hill Road, is a bit unusual for Cleveland in that it focuses on a small stable of local artists.

45

Busta's commitment to the development of the artists is comparable to galleries in larger art markets such as New York, Los Angeles and Chicago. Painters, print makers, sculptors, photographers and tapestry artists are represented individually in the gallery's eleven yearly shows.

Cleveland's downtown also contains numerous art galleries including **The Bonfoey Company,** which has served Cleveland for 98 years. The gallery specializes in 19th and 20th century paintings and prints, contemporary artwork, art restoration, carving and gilding, distinctive framing, fine art shipping, art consultations and appraisals.

The 9th Street Studio showcases the area's major fine artists. The studio is not limited to any style or medium and regularly displays glass art, paintings, sculptures, textiles and other art forms in a unique setting. The artwork is exhibited throughout one of Cleveland's oldest and most popular downtown restaurants, The New York Spaghetti House.

In the historic Warehouse District the **Brenda Kroos Gallery** displays the works of contemporary, nationally known artists. Paintings, fine art, limited editions and reproductions are included in the its six annual shows. The gallery also handles corporate sales and individual consultations. Owner Brenda Kroos, hoping to educate the public on contemporary art, encourages people to browse as they would in a museum.

While not precisely a gallery, also in the Warehouse District is **Wolf's Fine Art Auctioneers,** one of only ten fine arts auctioneers in the United States. The auction house holds 12 specialty auctions per year including an Important Art Glass and Decorative Arts Auction, a Prints and Drawing Auction, and an American and European Painting and Sculpture Auction.

Another noteworthy downtown gallery is **SPACES.** Founded in 1977, SPACES serves as a forum for avant-garde art in Northeast Ohio. The gallery creates opportunities for emerging local and regional artists to present their work to the public. SPACES exhibits any art that is new, unconventional and non-traditional, including video, film, dance, music, poetry, performance art and anything else that seems challenging.

In addition to those clustered in University Circle, Little Italy, and downtown, Cleveland has many other notable galleries dispersed throughout the area. **Vixseboxse Art Galleries** in Cleveland Heights is one of the area's oldest galleries dealing exclusively in 19th century and early 20th century fine art. This third generation run gallery owns most of its inventory of American and European paintings, watercolors and prints.

Scheele Galleries, also located in Cleveland Heights, handles primarily American artists and carries a wide variety of art forms. Special focuses of the gallery are nature and environmental art, and Cleveland School painters (circa 1900–1950). The gallery is helping to reestablish the national prominence of Frank Wilcox, Paul Travis, William Grauer, Henry Keller, William Sommer, Carl Gaertner and Clarence Carter. Contemporary local artists also are aggressively promoted.

Sylvia Ullman American Crafts Gallery focuses on the national art scene and exhibits primarily contemporary works. Established 26 years ago, it is one of the country's largest galleries and enjoys an outstanding national reputation. Special shows include Art in the Garden, the National Furniture Invitational, and the National Ceramic Invitational.

Eleven-year-old **Malcolm Brown Gallery,** in neighboring Shaker Heights, is a full service gallery renowned for quality art and service. It showcases artists of regional and national prominence including Romare Bearden, Elizabeth Catlett and Hughie Lee-Smith. Museum quality paintings, graphics, sculptures, and African contemporary pieces are on display during the gallery's eight annual shows.

The **Cleveland Center for Contemporary Art,** located in the Cleveland Play House, is celebrating its 23rd year of presenting nationally known contemporary artists. As the area's largest gallery, it considers public education and awareness of art an important part of its mission.

Sylvia Ullman

American Crafts Gallery

Sylvia Ullman
Amierican Crafts
Gallery
13010 Larchmere, in
the Shaker Square area

(216) 231-2008

The gallery intrigues; some pieces are deeply symbolic, some whimsical, but most cleverly combine the best of both attitudes.

With an extensive collection of creative handmade American crafts, this gallery is a magnet for collectors from across the country. Several hundred artists are represented in the gallery, which is among the most prestigious as well as one of the largest in the United States. But quality is not sacrificed for quantity — the watchword of the gallery is excellence. Only the finest functional and decorative pieces are carried.

The crafts themselves are contemporary works which reflect today's artistic trends, colors and forms. In this sense, the gallery is in constant flux, mirroring the evolution of both art and artist. As materials are refined and creative vision is redefined, Sylvia Ullman and Marilyn Bialosky are there to capture the essence of artistic expression and nurture young artists. "We have a personal relationship with 75% of the artists we represent."

With handmade American crafts being highly valued today by tradition-oriented consumers, the 25 year old gallery is thriving. Because of the respect and support offered by Sylvia and Marilyn, artists from across the country flock to the gallery with their works. Jewelry, decorative wall art, ceramics, fibers, sculpture, furniture, glass art, wood, mirrors, toys and games, and a myriad of other crafts are well represented throughout the year. Seasonally, the gallery holds four shows: the National Ceramic Invitational, Art in a Garden, the National Furniture Invitational, and the Holiday Collectible Show.

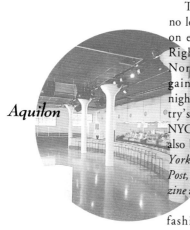

Aquilon

The East and West Coasts no longer hold the monopoly on entertainment hot spots. Right here on America's North Coast, Aquilon is gaining fame as a stellar nightclub, one of the country's top five, according to NYC's *Paper Magazine.* It has also been featured in the *New York Daily News, New York Post, Mademoiselle, Self Magazine* and *USA Today.*

On the cutting edge in fashion, art and music, Aquilon is also on the edge of the picturesque Cuyahoga River and in the heart of the Flats, Cleveland's lively entertainment district. Conceived by Cleveland native Angela VerDuyn, the club was designed by New York architect Jeffrey G. Beers. Charlie Merrill is co-owner.

The nightclub, open only on Saturdays, offers an interesting mix. From 8:30 to midnight, a 19-piece Big Band Orchestra brings back the flavor of the Forties. Starting at midnight, guest DJ's from around the world spin avant-garde dance music until 4 am.

Aquilon boasts an astonishing 15-martini menu starring the Sake and the Blue Sapphire. The club also hosts a Late Night Breakfast from 2 to 3:30 when customized omelettes and waffles are offered.

Wednesdays, Fridays and Sundays, Aquilon has an alter ego, "The Lift," for the progressive dance crowd.

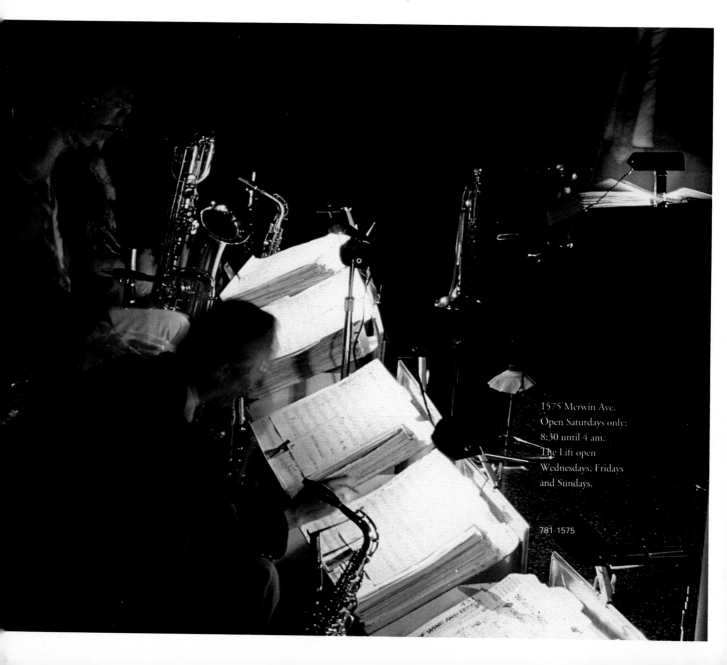

1575 Merwin Ave.
Open Saturdays only:
8:30 until 4 am.
The Lift open
Wednesdays, Fridays
and Sundays.

781-1575

by Van McCulloch

Dining in Cleveland is whatever you choose. Haute cuisine . . . downhome delicious . . . sophisticated . . . casual . . . American regional . . . Continental . . . eclectic. There is, in fact, no typical dining experience in Cleveland. The city's very diversity — its ethnic and cultural pluralism — is showcased in its dining establishments, where the world's great culinary disciplines are all represented.

While this unparalleled variety defies easy characterization, it may explain why Cleveland restaurants hold such strong appeal for visitors. And vigorous competition in Cleveland's restaurant industry assures consistently high levels of quality, both at the inexpensive eatery and the pricey restaurant. Those hungering for a spirited setting

and casual menu will not be disappointed. Gratification also awaits the gourmet seeking classic cuisine in an upscale ambiance of crystal goblets and tableside preparation.

And for those in-the-know, evenings come alive at nightspots ranging from intimate piano bars to New York-style clubs.

Welcome, then, to the wide and wonderful world of Cleveland dining. Whatever your pleasure, seek and you shall find.

...e most discriminating of tastes

Dining
&
Nightlife

Classics

Photography by
Beth Segal

The Burgess Grand Cafe

At The Burgess Grand Cafe, "grand" is not just a word; it's a philosophy. Grand is the quintessence of fine dining. Elegant presentation of food. Splendid surroundings. A reminder of an era when perfect service was taken for granted.

Just a short walk from Public Square in the historic Warehouse District, the restaurant is a popular rendezvous for Clevelanders. They are attracted by a wide-ranging menu including Northern Italian dishes with freshly made pasta, duck breast, sweetbreads, fresh seafood and filet of tenderloin. A cellar well-stocked with domestic and imported wines adds to the enjoyment.

Even the regulars never tire of the beautiful surroundings. They dine on tables topped with imported rose-colored marble; sip from black stemmed wine goblets; admire the provocative wall murals that were commissioned by the proprietor, Paul Martoccia.

Breakfast, usually an elusive meal, is not only available here, it's a work of art. Offerings like Oatmeal Pecan Pancakes and Orange Brandied French Toast give a special jumpstart to the power breakfast. A bountiful Sunday Brunch is also available.

Light menus are featured in the lounge where a jazz trio performs Wednesday, Friday and Saturday evenings.

Reservations are recommended for those who want to experience this eminently upscale establishment.

1406 W.6th
Serving breakfast &
lunch Mon.-Fri.
Dinner 7 days a week,
starting at 5:30 pm
Sunday Brunch from
11 to 3.

574-2232

Paul Martoccia, proprietor

Donna Chriszt, executive chef

"Come and find out why it

took a lifetime to create

The Burgess Grand Cafe."

Paul Martoccia, Proprietor

Cleveland's Karamu
House, founded in
1915, was the first
interracial cultural
arts center in the
United States.

Watermark

1250 Old River Road
in the Flats
Lunch Mon.-Fri.
11:30 am–2:30 pm
Dinner Sun.-Thurs.
5:30–10 pm; Fri.&
Sat. 5:30–Midnight
Brunch Sat.& Sun.
11:30 am–2:30 pm
Valet parking available

241-1600

Hap Gray,

general manager

estaurant

The legions of regulars who frequent the Watermark know they can count on one thing – that the restaurant is never the same place twice. Spectacular scenery, viewed from indoors or from the River Patio, is an ever-changing kaleidoscope of activity and watercraft. The menu also is changed every day to reflect the freshest bounties of the marketplace.

With the same certainty, patrons know too that some things never change. The kitchen takes uncompromising pride in food preparation; no short cuts here. Everything from bread and salad dressings to devastating desserts is prepared "from scratch" on the premises. Also ever-present is the ambiance of laid-back, casual elegance.

As befits a riverfront restaurant, impeccably fresh fish and seafood are kings of the menu and the kitchen gives preferential treatment to its royalty. Delicacies such as mahi mahi, grouper, trout, fresh tuna or shrimp may be sauteed, baked or marinated, then gently grilled on smoky-sweet mesquite. Landlubbers can find friendly fare, too, on a menu that is stunning in its scope and variety. Prices are surprisingly moderate for food and service of such unwavering quality.

The wine list, one of Cleveland's most extensive, concentrates on California whites to complement the seafood. The list has earned numerous awards and made the Watermark a favorite among local wine connoisseurs. Bottles are attractively displayed in expansive racks behind the bar.

A startlingly incongruous combination of design elements makes for an interesting atmosphere here. The historic warehouse milieu of exposed pipes and rafters gives customers a sense of yesterday, when industry ruled the Flats' riverfront. The Flats today, however, are about fun and frolic. Whimsical touches at the Watermark, like the sailboat extended sideways over the bar, symbolize the lighthearted mood of today.

at The Galleria
at Erieview
E. 9th St. & St. Clair
Ave.

696-CAFE

Serving lunch
11:30-3:30 Mon.-Sat.
Dinner 5-10 pm
Mon.–Thurs., till
midnight Fri. & Sat.
Open Sunday from 11
to 6.

Gary Lucarelli,
owner

Sweetwater's

Cafe Sausalito

When Clevelanders are hungry for a large helping of fun with their food, you'll find them at Sweetwater's Cafe Sausalito. Gary Lucarelli's establishment is known as "The Sardi's of Cleveland," a description coined by local newspaper columnist, Mary Strassmeyer. Dining here is indeed a theatrical experience.

Even its location is dramatic. Curved front windows overlook a busy interior street in The Galleria, downtown's spectacular glass-enclosed mall. Sausalito's stucco walls, copper accents and glazed quarry tile give coastal flavor to the restaurant, named for the famous California art colony.

Writing on table cloths, a basic no-no in more formal places, is not just tolerated here, it is actually encouraged. Tables are covered with drawing paper and crayons are provided for artistic doodlers. Theatre-goers applaud the restaurant's dinner/theatre packages and those holding tickets either for Playhouse Square or The Cleveland Play House relish rides in Sausalito's nostalgic double decker bus.

Innovative foods, starring "tapas" (which can serve as mini-entrees), appeal to the munch-and-mingle crowd. Also popular on the extensive menu are such house specialties as Paella Sausalito, a savory Spanish casserole and San Francisco Cioppino, a zesty peasant fisherman's soup. A library of fine wines is displayed on a rear wall and gourmet takeout is available at the Pronto window which, by the way, offers a look at a truly spotless kitchen.

This is definitely a place where the fun-loving set, theatre-bound or not, can unwind and savor coastal cuisine. Valet parking is available.

Getty's at the Hanna/Getty's West

Two restaurants — one famous name

Legendary among locals and increasingly among sophisticated visitors, the two restaurants named Getty's help define the meaning of truly fine dining in Cleveland. The Carmel brothers, Todd and Donn, blend three decades of experience into a single and unwavering commitment to quality both at Getty's at the Hanna and Getty's in Westlake.

In the heart of Cleveland's Playhouse Square, Getty's at the Hanna presents an appropriately dramatic decor. Fluted columns support a high ceiling decorated with Hellenic-Romanesque characters and etched glass partitions create the intimacy of dining alcoves. During intermissions at the three theatres just across the street, many playgoers patronize the Chicago-style bar. Dinner-theatre packages are offered and an after-theatre menu is available. Todd Carmel is the proprietor of this popular downtown rendezvous where patrons are entertained by jazz pianists

Tuesday through Sunday during lunch and dinner.

Getty's West, where Donn Carmel presides, has a relaxing, hospitable ambiance. Depending on the weather, alfresco dining may be savored on the quaint summer patio or guests may watch TV on the giant screen in the lounge.

The two establishments feature many of the same favorite dishes. Eclectic menus stress the chef's daily creations and several entree salads. Salad Brittany, for one, tops a bed of bibb lettuce and radicchio with grilled chicken, bacon, almonds and a warm French brandy dressing. Dinner entrees include a number of beef dishes such as Blackened Strip Steak. Getty's is also famous for superb entrees like Veal St. Jacques, Chicken Marsala, Pasta Primavera and the Daily Fresh Catch.

Getty's boasts a large wine cellar as well as an outstanding selection of port and cognac.

Getty's at the Hanna
1422 Euclid Ave. at
Playhouse Square
Open for lunch
Mon.–Fri. 11–2:30
Dinner Mon.-Sat.
starting at 5 pm Open
Sundays for major
theatre events only.

771-1818

Getty's West
25651 Detroit Rd.,
Westlake
Open for lunch
Mon.–Fri. 11–2:30
Dinner: Mon.–Thurs.
5–11; Fri. & Sat. 5–12
Open Sunday 4–10 pm

835-9332

Todd and Donn Carmel, proprietors

Ristorante Barbarino's of Gordon Square

"delightfully, differently

Italian . . . and more"

Carlos Colon
and Sam Gliozzi,
partners.

6504 Detroit Ave.
Open for lunch
Monday through
Friday. Open for
dinner seven days a
week.

651-5551

A visit to Ristorante Barbarino's is a delicious departure from the ordinary. The slogan, "delightfully, differently Italian . . . and more," rather effectively says it all.

A menu that offers both regional and classical Italian dishes, all prepared to order, is a "delight" to fans of Italian food. "Different" is defined by a creative, free-spirited menu that reflects the chef's inventiveness. Exotic pasta, salad dressings, cheesecake and ice cream, all made on the premises, give meaning to the words . . ."and more."

As patrons stroll through the door, they should expect to be welcomed as an old friend by Carlos Colon. He and co-owner Salvatore "Sam" Gliozzi view the restaurant as a hands-on venture and prefer to treat customers as guests in their own home.

Sam extends the hands-on philosophy to the kitchen where he enjoys experimenting with subtle new combinations of fresh herbs and olive oil. One of his creations, a salad dressing with tuna fish — Tonnato — became so popular that it is now the house dressing. Also a long-running favorite is Sam's version of Fettucine Verde — spinach/tomato fettucine and charbroiled chicken breast tossed with olive oil and vegetables. It is one of many entrees providing a tasty alternative to the health-conscious among us.

Those wishing to experience the congenial service and creative cuisine are advised to plan ahead. Reservations are suggested as the often full house at Ristorante Barbarino's is testimony to its success.

Classics

Classics — a name not casually bestowed. A name signifying tradition. Refinement. Excellence that withstands the test of time.

Classics, then, is the perfect name for a restaurant that treats dining as a hallowed art form . . . for an establishment that is clearly one of the most opulent in the entire area. Located in the world-renowned Clinic Center Hotel, Classics is accustomed to hosting celebrities and royalty from around the world. It is also the only Cleveland restaurant that AAA has judged worthy of its Four-Diamond rating.

A classic menu disregards transient trends in favor of fresh, satisfying food that is always in fashion. Special entrees include Pike Fillet, Tournedos Henry IV and Chicken Veronique. The appetizers are extraordinary and the desserts irresistible. Guests are pampered with such royal treatment as complimentary valet parking and tableside preparation by tuxedo-clad servers, a signature tradition at Classics.

Diners are serenaded by piano and strings in a flower-filled setting that somehow induces relaxation amid all the elegance. Advance registration and proper attire are required.

Carnegie at E. 96th St.
Clinic Center Hotel
Serving lunch
Monday through
Friday 11:30-2:30
Dinner Monday
through Thursday
5:30-10 Friday &
Saturday 5:30-10:30
Closed on Sunday.

791-1300

Photography provided by
Nesnadny & Schwartz
except as indicated below:

p. 4 Hedrich-Blessing.

p. 6 Upper right; T. Williams,
Image Finders.

p. 7 Hedrich-Blessing.

p. 8 Lower left; Jim Baron,
Image Finders.

p. 9 Upper left; Jim Baron,
Image Finders.

p. 14-15 Upper center; Jim
Baron, Baron Photography.

p. 15 George Remington.

p. 17 Lower center, left; Scott
McDonald © Hedrich-Blessing.

p. 19 Center right; Benjamin
Margalite, Cleveland.

p. 21 Hedrich-Blessing.

p. 23 Lower left; Jim Baron,
Baron Photography.

p. 26 Upper left; Jim Baron,
Baron Photography.

p. 37 Center right; John
Markowski.

p. 38 Upper left; Michael
Edwards.

p. 39 Upper; Michael Edwards.

p. 40-41 Jim Baron,
Baron Photography.

p. 42 Jim Baron, Baron
Photography.

p. 43 Roger Schreiber.

p. 46-47 Jim Baron,
Baron Photography.

p. 48 Upper left; Roger
Mastroianni.

p. 49 Ralph Gibson.

p. 59 Full page; Jim Baron,
Baron Photography. Inset;
Beth Segal.

p. 63 Jim Baron, Image Finders.

p. 66-67 Sybia Franklin,
Image Finders.

p. 72-73 H. Stata, Image
Finders.

p. 74 Metropolitan Zoo.

p. 75 Eric Hanson, Remington
Studios.

p. 76-77 Center spread; Eric
Hanson, Remington Studios.

p. 84 Upper and lower; Jim
Baron, Baron Photography.

p. 86 Center; Hedrich-Blessing.

p. 96 ©Jennie Jones.

Inside back cover Hedrich-
Blessing

Whether you're "In Cleveland" or not,

enjoy the book that

showcases the city's finest.

Additional copies can be ordered by calling

1-800-234-2454, 9 to 5 EST,

Monday through Friday.

$18.95 per copy; quantity discounts available;

Visa, Master Card, American Express.

Published by City Visitor, P.O. Box 612, Hudson, Ohio 44236.

Choice Excursions

Adventures and

entertainment, from

glitz to grandeur,

await the

would-be explorer

Cleveland is a city waiting to be discovered. And, much to the delight of newcomers, this big city with a small town passion is a gracious host. Cleveland is a city of water and lights, bridges and skyscrapers, museums and churches. And, as we who live on the North Coast can attest, a day of traipsing in and around Cleveland is bound to be enjoyable for tourists and Clevelanders alike.

All major metropolitan cities offer unique buildings, interesting architecture, historical firsts and "things to see and do." Cleveland is no different. Granted, Cleveland may not have the worldly airs of a New York or the big city reputation of Chicago, but it does boast the dynamics of the "Big Apple" and the eats and treats of the "Windy City" in hospitable portions, with ease of access as a bonus.

From the world-renowned Cleveland Orchestra to the bustling ethnic pockets of life encircling the city, Cleveland entertains. From the spectacular to the ordinary — Cleveland is alive.

Downtown

The burgeoning downtown area is in the midst of redefining its skyline. Bold new structures are intermingled with the solid, architectural stalwarts of an earlier era. The following represent a combination of landmark attractions and interesting asides.

Tower City Center With the sixty-year-old Terminal Tower as its centerpiece, a once-defunct train station has been transformed into a sleek, glass-encased showpiece of world-class retail and sophisticated eateries.

Public Square The true center of the city, the Public Square quadrants showcase the city's founder, General Moses Cleaveland, SW; progressive Mayor Thomas L. Johnson, NW; and the Soldiers and Sailors Monument, SE. Cleveland's Public Square was the first in the country to display a Christmas tree in 1851.

Old Stone Church Built in 1855, it is the oldest existing church in downtown. Stained glass windows by Tiffany, a wooden barrel-vaulted ceiling and oak paneling create an awe-inspiring presence.

by Ann M. Zoller

Ohio ranks fourth in the nation in number of wineries.

The Flats, Cleveland's famous entertainment mecca.

BP America Building This 46-story granite structure and its protruding glass atrium sit on the southeast corner of Public Square. A dramatic water cascade in the atrium serves as a popular backdrop for Saturday afternoon bridal parties.

The Arcade This 100-year-old, five-story arcade is the largest — and possibly the grandest — in the United States. Glass skylights look down on marble staircases and brass railings in this unique architectural beauty. Today, the Arcade is home to offices, shops and restaurants.

Cleveland Public Library/ Eastman Garden Cleveland's is the largest public library in Northeast Ohio and one of the largest open-shelf libraries in the U.S. with over 6.5 million volumes. The Eastman Garden is cloaked between the library's two main buildings. Named in honor of Linda Eastman, Director of the Cleveland Public Library from 1918 – 1938, this idyllic respite is a popular lunchtime escape for many downtown workers.

Cleveland City Hall Dedicated on July 4, 1916, the Cleveland City Hall is classi-cally designed in gray granite. The Rotunda or main lobby of the building features the "Spirit of '76" painting by Archibald Willard.

The Galleria and Towers at Erieview Natural sunlight showers the two stories of this glittering, glass shopping plaza. The airy, sophisticated mall features fine designer shops, restaurants and a food court.

North Point Buildings Occupying an enviable vantage point at the corner of Lakeside Avenue and East 9th Street, North Point is the headquarters of Jones, Day, Reavis & Pogue — the world's second largest law firm.

The Halle Building Converted from the former Halle Department Store to offices and retail space in 1985, The Halle Building was one of the first to bring specialty retail back to downtown Cleveland.

North Coast Harbor Over $11 million dollars was invested in transforming 7.6 acres into this lakefront park and harbor. Visitors in the summer will enjoy the finger-licking fun of many city events at the site. Future plans for $1 billion in new development call for a maritime museum, his-

toric shipyard, world-class aquarium, theater, retail shops and a hotel.

Playhouse Square Center One of Cleveland's proudest jewels, Playhouse Square boasts three magnificently restored 1920 epic theaters — the Ohio, State and Palace. Capacity crowds rise to their feet to applaud the Cleveland Ballet, Great Lakes Theater Festival, Cleveland Opera and visiting performances — from cabaret-style to full-scale Broadway productions. Bravo!

Flats/Nautica

The Flats! Cleveland has developed a new national reputation on the mystique, excitement and distinctive character of this low-lying expanse along the Cuyahoga River. With a natural ambience which could not be created, the Flats must be experienced. The glitz of flashing neon is thrown against the raw power of massive ore boats commanding the crooks and bends of the winding Cuyahoga amidst a labyrinth of moving bridges unlike any in the country. With nearly forty nightclubs, bars and restaurants packed along the teeming riverbanks, the Flats is uniquely designed to accommodate all. On any typical summer weekend, over 120,000 revelers will follow the call to the Flats. The river itself is a hotbed of activity as sailboats, rowing teams and the gaudy powerboat crowd posture for the chance to see and be seen.

The east bank of the Flats offers a potpourri of sensory delights. From the haute cui-

The old-world-style West Side Market

sine at the posh Sammy's to the boilermaker crowd at Biggie's Crooked River Saloon, a stroll down Old River Road is a true adventure. Hot spots include the Watermark Restaurant, known for its fresh "sophisticated" seafood, casual elegance and riverfront patio; the River's Edge, a beer drinkers delight with an international deli; Noisemakers, where the 18 and up crowd go to bump and grind amidst high decibels and flashing lights; Fagan's, one of the Flats' firsts, recently remodeled with expanded deck and menu — great for the "Happy Hour" crowd; Aquilon — Big Band Saturday nights fill the trendy dance floors; the Flat Iron Cafe, an Irish pub where longshoremen rub elbowswith the young and fashionable.

Nautica, a multi-faceted entertainment complex, encompasses the entire west bank of the Flats. Two imposing jackknife bridges mark the parameters of the complex as a fitting salute to the industrial roots of the Flats, which allows for the paradox of sights and sounds experienced today. The Nautica Stage, an impressive 4,000-seat, outdoor amphitheatre, is perched on the riverbank at the southern tip of the project. The Cleveland skyline provides a spectacular backdrop for the passing of 900 foot ore boats dwarfing the stage and amazing national entertainers in mid-performance.

Adjacent to the stage is the recently renovated Powerhouse, a dramatic architectural gem which originally powered the city's electric rail system. The exposed brick and expansive atria serve as a gorgeous rustic home to T.G.I Friday's; the Improv, the country's best-known laugh house; Powerplay, a high-tech gameroom, bar and diner with an emphasis on fun, high-volumed competition; Grand Slam Grille, a sports-theme restaurant with memorabilia from the highs and lows in Cleveland sports; Windows on the River, a private catering facility; and many specialty retail shops.

A little bit further down the half-mile boardwalk, one finds Club Coconuts, a glitzy, glass-fronted nightclub where synchronized props, movable palm trees, and pulsing video walls dazzle the huge dance floor.

Next, it's Jillian's Billiard Club. The emphasis here is on Billiard Club — not pool hall. The decidedly sophisticated club features thirty tables in an opulent setting full of rich woods and designer touches. A casual yet innovative menu makes this stop a different and totally enjoyable diversion.

At the end of the boardwalk is Shooters Waterfront Cafe U.S.A. An endless array of powerboats, yachts, poolside posers and wandering tourists make this a prime spot for people watching. An eclectic menu taps all favorites and attracts thousands to this Florida-born hot spot.

Far and Near

Cleveland's West Side Market sits at the doorstep of Ohio City and should not be missed. This old-world-style indoor and outdoor market presents a delectable slice of life reminiscent of an earlier era. Over 100 merchants representing virtually all of Cleveland's ethnic pockets peddle fresh produce, meats, cheese and baked goods in dynamic chaos.

Just east of University Circle lies yet another testament to Cleveland's deep ethnic roots. Little Italy has preserved the timeless essence of "the neighborhood" as only

The Cleveland Play House

an authentic Italian community can. Brick streets are rich with tempting aromas and jammed with houses, bistros, bakeries, churches and galleries which make for amusing browsing and excellent eating!

The NASA Lewis Research Center is located near Cleveland Hopkins International Airport in Brookpark and displays the history and milestones of space exploration and everyday uses of space technology. Tours of lab facilities and special programs are

Shamu, star of Sea World

Thrilling shows at Sea World.

Kids love Shamu. And vice versa.

Sea World of Ohio is both highly entertaining and educational — a great place for a family adventure.

available by appointment. Other exhibits are open to the public Monday – Sunday. 2100 Brookpark Road. 433-2001.

The southwestern shores of Lake Erie, roughly an hour's drive from Cleveland, are commonly referred to as Wine Country. There some of the state's finest vineyards produce a variety of award-winning wines. The natural basin-like effect of the lake makes for ideal growing conditions throughout much of the state's northwest region. Tours of wineries are available and many have quaint eateries or restaurants on the grounds making for a delightful excursion. 800/227-6972.

The Lake Erie Islands attract thousands of visitors year-round. Located off the northwestern shores of the state, the Islands are but a ferry ride away and offer an unusual conglomeration of sights and sounds which are sure to please. Of the four islands — Kelley's Island, North Bass Island, Middle Bass Island and South Bass Island — the latter is the most popular, known simply as Put-in-Bay. Once on the island, bicycle and golf cart rentals simplify the abundant opportunities for sightseeing. Of historical significance is Perry's Monument, commemorating the end of the War of 1812 which followed a dramatic victory in the Battle of Lake Erie. The monument was erected in 1912 as a symbol of the friendship enjoyed by the United States and Canada. Tours of the island and its local wineries, quaint shops, a variety of restaurants, pubs, festivals and an active boating population make this getaway an ideal escape.

Several local companies offer guided tours of the Cleveland area. Trolley Tours of Cleveland offers sleekly designed trolleys which may be used as full tour packages or simply as inspired transportation. The Goodtime III offers river and lake cruises which are both informative and fun. Executive Arrangements and North Coast Tours are firms which specialize in the coordination of tours and itineraries for special groups or conventions.

Squeal Appeal

Northeast Ohio is in the enviable position of having three major amusement parks just a short drive away. Sea World of Ohio, Geagua Lake and Cedar Point Amusement Park are all national attractions within easy reach of the Cleveland market.

Sea World of Ohio is a great place for a family adventure which is both highly entertaining and educational. Children and adults of all ages will love the feature shows, educational exhibits and attractions which foster understanding and appreciation of marine animals. Sea World is a beautifully landscaped 90-acre marine life park and family showplace unique to mid-America. Being one of only four in the country, it attracts thousands from throughout the region. With six live shows and more than 20 attractions and exhibits,

Northeast Ohio

is in the enviable

position of having

three major

amusement

parks just a

short drive away.

Sea World is a wonderful escape for the whole family. 1-800-63-SHAMU.

Neighboring Geagua Lake has more than 100 rides and attractions, including Turtle Beach's Totally Expanded Kid-Kontrolled Amphibious Action Area for children. Other features include 4 roller coasters, the Wave, live shows and restaurants. 1-800-THE-WAVE.

One hour west of Cleveland is Cedar Point Amusement Park. The world's fastest and highest roller coaster, the Magnum XL-200, is one of the 9 roller coasters and sixty rides in the 164-acre park. 419/626-0830.

Sidestreets

From Tower City Center to University Circle, Cleveland boasts a host of worldly attractions. Yet just as engaging are those interesting oddities found slightly off the beaten path. From the Heights to the Flats and beyond, Cleveland is bursting with well-kept secrets. These are the nooks and crannies of a city cherished by those who live it.

Federal Reserve Bank The Federal Reserve Bank in Cleveland contains the largest vault door in the world in a classically designed building of pink sienna marble. Statues of *Security* and *Integrity* along the East 6th Street entrance have been known to don Browns' football helmets during the passion of the playoffs. Matinee idol Francis X. Bushman posed for artist H. Hering, who carved the elaborate statues. For tours, 579-2125.

Terminal Tower Observation Deck Some of the most spectacular views of the city are afforded from the 42nd story of the Terminal Tower. The Observation Deck is open 11:00 a.m. – 4:00 p.m. on weekends and holidays. Admission is charged. 621-7981.

U.S.S. Cod A World War II submarine which survived seven patrols in the South Pacific (some lasted as long as 63 days) is on permanent display at the north end of East 9th Street. No admission is charged, although donations are accepted for the Save the Cod Foundation, which keeps the Cod in Cleveland. 566-8770.

Lakeview Cemetery President James A. Garfield's monument and John D. Rockefeller's grave share this beautiful Eden-like cemetery with many other Cleveland history makers. The Jeptha Wade Memorial Chapel, replete with glass and window mosaics designed by Louis Tiffany, is another highlight. Located at 12316 Euclid Avenue, or enter at the top of Mayfield Road Hill at Kenilworth Road.

Cedar Point Amusement Park

Brandywine Falls The National Parks System's recently completed $750,000 wood walkway makes this falls one of the most spectacular in Ohio. Located in the Cuyahoga Valley on Akron-Peninsula Road in Peninsula. **Holden Arboretum** On 2,900 acres of varied terrain, this living museum contains 15,000 varieties of trees, shrubs and vines from around the world; six ponds; a sugar maple house and harvesting;

73

wild deer and geese; picnicking, hiking and cross country skiing; a museum; a library; and gift shop in this nature lovers' paradise. Located at 9500 Sperry Road in Mentor. 946-4400.

Euclid Tavern This authentic neighborhood bar showcases some of Cleveland's finest bands and musicians. Its down-to-earth blues bar atmosphere provided the perfect location for the Michael J. Fox film *Light of Day* in 1986. 11629 Euclid Avenue 229-7788.

Great Lakes Brewing Company Cleveland's only brewery and Ohio's first brew pub offers a variety of seasonal brews which are prepared in full view in this unique turn-of-the-century Ohio City eatery. An elaborate, hand-carved mahogany bar — Cleveland's oldest working bar — is said to boast a hole from a bullet intended for the "untouchable" Eliot Ness, who once served as Cleveland Safety Director and frequented the establishment. Located at 2516 Market Avenue. 771-4404.

Amish Country To the east of Cleveland in Geauga County lie the quaint Amish communities. Visitors will enjoy the sights and sounds of horse-drawn buggies and are welcome to visit authentic restaurants, antique shops, country stores and watch special seasonal demonstrations, such as cider pressing in the fall. U.S. Routes 322 and 422 and State Route 87 in Geauga County.

Coventry A unique assortment of coffee houses, outdoor cafes, bistros, exotic little shops and galleries. Cleveland's own Rive Gauche, located at Coventry and Euclid Heights Roads in Cleveland Heights.

Cultural Gardens The Cleveland Cultural Gardens represent 19 major ethnic groups which are dominant in the area. The first garden, the Shakespeare Garden (later renamed the British Garden) opened in 1916 and inspired the series which was dedicated as a unit in 1939. Each garden reflects the culture of the nationality through the landscape and sculptures represented. Located from St. Clair Avenue to East 105th Street on Martin Luther King, Jr. Drive.

Heisman House Home where John Heisman, for whom the Heisman Trophy was named, was born and raised. In Ohio City on Bridge Avenue at West 29th Street.

Dunham Tavern Museum This former residence, constructed in the 1820s, was a frequent stop on the Buffalo-Cleveland-Detroit stagecoach. Now a museum that recreates an early Cleveland tavern with original wood floorings, pioneer tools, toys and samplers. Closed Mondays. 6709 Euclid Avenue. 431-1060.

Brush Arc Lamp Mounted outside John Q's Public Bar and Grill, the Brush Arc Lamp Plaque displays a replica of the original Arc Lamp designed by Charles F. Brush. Cleveland's Public Square was the first in the world to be lit by electricity on April 29, 1879.

Lawnfield Home of the 20th President, James A. Garfield. This thirty-room Victorian home displays the lifestyles of three generations of the Garfield family. Garfield acquired the house in 1876 and conducted the first successful "front porch" campaign as more than 17,000 people from all over the country came by train to listen to him speak from the porch. Located off I-90 on Rte. 20 off the Rte. 306 exit. 255-8722.

The Cleveland Metroparks Zoo

Athletic diversions, both for the spectator and participant,

are enjoyed vigorously here in Cleveland.

The Playing Fields

Here in Cleveland, sports fanaticism is nearly epidemic. It's easy to pursue a favorite avocation, either as a spellbound spectator or a passionate participant.

Cleveland plays in the big leagues, with franchises in every major professional sport: the Cleveland Indians (American League baseball), the Cleveland Browns (National Football League), the Cleveland Cavaliers (National Basketball Association) and the Cleveland Crunch (Major Soccer League).

Those wishing to take a more active role in sports are also in an enviable situation. Cleveland is noteworthy for having an abundance of facilities where indoor athletic

pursuits and such outdoor activities as golf and water sports can be enjoyed.

And happily, all Clevelanders find themselves in a setting that is most unique for an urban milieu. The bustling city is nestled between two major park systems: Lakefront State Park along Lake Erie, and the Cleveland Metroparks network, fondly known as the "Emerald Necklace." This open space enriches the quality of life by providing respite from the daily grind, and in its extraordinary acreage a multitude of outdoor activities flourish.

Major league sports, of course, attract the largest, most passionate crowds. The venerable Municipal Stadium

Half of the population
of North America lives
within 600 miles of
Cleveland.

Boston Mills Ski Resort, a favorite winter playground

stands tall among our country's traditional fields of competition — a symbol of Cleveland's historic role in professional sports. With seating for 80,000, it is also among the largest in the United States. The stadium's heyday may be waning, however, as plans are moving along on a project called Gateway. The multi-purpose sports complex is designed to include a modern baseball stadium with seating expansion for football. While the ambitious project symbolizes the willingness of the citizenry to adapt to change and prepare for the future, the Stadium's legacy will endure.

Wherever games are played, or whatever the team's fortunes at any given moment, Clevelanders remain loyal to the Indians, their own "Tribe", one of only three charter teams left in the American League.

Loyalty to the Cleveland Browns is also fervent. The team is traditionally one of the strongest in the NFL. A major factor on the Cleveland scene for more than 40 years,

the Browns have graduated a dozen superstars to the Pro Football Hall of Fame located nearby in Canton, Ohio. Browns mania grips all of Northeast Ohio during football season, and despite Ohio's fickle and sometime frigid weather, nearly every game at Municipal Stadium is a sellout.

Strong contenders in the NBA, the Cavaliers provide many heart-stopping moments for basketball fans at the Richfield Coliseum. Also doing battle at the Coliseum, the Crunch is Cleveland's newest professional team. Many young soccer players are among the devotees of this fast-growing sport.

While Cleveland's status as a mecca for professional teams is almost without peer, the variety of other sports activities available to spectators and weekend athletes is also exceptional. Turf fans cheer on their favorite thoroughbreds at Thistledown Race Track or enjoy harness racing at Northfield Park. Thousands of benchwarmers share in the excitement of Indy-style rac-

ing at the Budweiser Cleveland Grand Prix on its 220-mile course at Cleveland's Burke Lakefront Airport. The nation's oldest air show, the Cleveland National, is also held at Burke Lakefront Airport.

Winter offers a host of seasonal opportunities for the hardy souls in our midst. Options include sledding, ice skating, tobogganing and skiing — both downhill and cross-country. Racquetball and tennis are enjoying a remarkable growth in popularity matcherd by an ever-increasing number of public courts and private clubs. Cleveland is regularly the site of top pro and amateur tennis tournaments. The city also hosts many local and statewide softball contests, and a number of tourneys sponsored by the Pro Bowling Association.

Cleveland is also a place where nature lovers can rejoice. While most municipalities have some open spaces, this city is almost fanatic about it. Newcomers are astonished to learn that

The variety of activities available to the weekend athlete is exceptional.

Bike trails meander through the Cleveland Metroparks.

they can escape the metropolitan maelstrom and find
the respite and renewal of
greenspace within 15 minutes
of anywhere in Cleveland.

This enviable urban park
system includes 18,000 acres
of unspoiled woodland
stretching from the North
Chagrin Reservation on the
east to Rocky River on the
west side. Along with the
Metroparks Zoo, this
"Emerald Necklace" encircles
the city on three sides. More
than 80 miles of scenic park
roadways connect the 12 parks
known as "reservations."

Variety is the watchword
in this expanse of natural
beauty. Wildlife and water-
fowl find sanctuary among
hiking, biking and bridle
trails. There are picnic areas
and nature centers. Golf
courses and playfields. Lakes
for fishing, swimming and
boating. Cross-country ski
trails, hills for sledding and
refrigerated chutes for tobogganing. There is even a photography club.

Five Nature Centers pro-
vide visitors information and
entertainment. Massive shale
cliffs rise above the willows,
and all-purpose trails meander
through the valleys. Turkey
buzzards, observing their
innate and predictable time
clock, return to roost at
Hinckley Reservation on the
Ides of March every year.

Following through the
Bedford Reservation is
Tinker's Creek, named for a
member of the surveying
party headed by Moses
Cleaveland, whose name,
slightly altered, now graces a
major American city. Tinker's
Creek has cut a deep-walled
gorge, declared a National
Natural Landmark, that
boasts an unmatched wild-
flower display every spring.
The scenic overlook on the
Gorge Parkway offers a vis-
taunrivaled anywhere north of
the Smoky Mountains.

At the South Chagrin
Reservation is the Metro-
politan Polo Field, head-
quarters of the Cleveland Polo
Club. The venerable sport is
enjoying a renaissance in this
country, and fans champion
their favorite teams at matches
held on Sunday afternoons.
The field is also used by dog
clubs and for horse shows,
including the prestigious
Hunter-Jumper Classic, highlight of the oldest equestrian
Grand Prix in America.

For animal lovers, trips
around the world depart daily
at the Cleveland Metroparks
Zoo, the tenth oldest in the

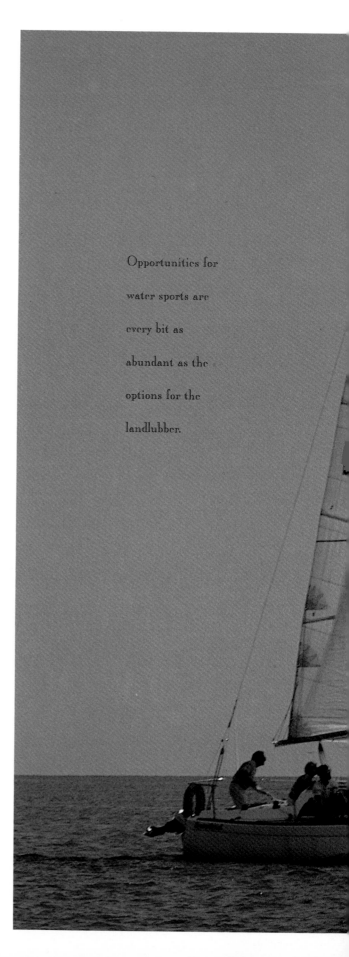

Opportunities for

water sports are

every bit as

abundant as the

options for the

landlubber.

country. Visitors stroll through the natural setting of the Birds of the World exhibit. Explore underwater sea life including sharks, piranhas, sting rays and living coral. Walk on the plains of Africait. Explore underwater sea life including sharks, piranhas, sting rays and living coral. Walk on the plains of Africa where tall grass and a dry moat are all that separates visitors from the wild inhabitants. Tired? Jump on a free Zoo Train or the Outback Railroad for a trip down under through Australia. More than 3,000 animals occupy the 165 picturesque, wooded area.

Cleveland Metroparks also operate six golf courses, ranging from a par three and an executive course to championship layouts that challenge even the best of golfers. Three of them: Big Met, Little Met and Mastick Woods, are located in Rocky River Reservation. Sleepy Hollow is in Brecksville, Shawnee Hills in Bedford and Manakiki, thechampionship course (a real challenge!), is located in Willoughby Hills. From mid-March through mid-November, the courses are open daily from dawn to dusk.

The six are among an astonishing number of public and private courses in the area. Nearly 300 courses beautify the Northern Ohio landscape where the natural mix of rolling hills, flat expanses and verdant forests is the stuff of dreams for a golf course architect.

While the profusion of courses is remarkable, there is good reason: avid interest in the sport is par for the course as Clevelanders spend more money on golf, per capita, than do residents of any other city in the country.

Golf is also a spectator sport here. Numerous PGA tournaments are staged in Northern Ohio, including the NEC World Series of Golf and the Ameritech Senior Open. Regional PGA organizations also sponsor opens for their member pros, tournaments that customarily offer a free opportunity to study the techniques of non-celebrity pros.

One area golf course, Quail Hollow, has hosted a number of major tournaments, including United States Amateur Qualifiers, the Ohio Open and the Northern Ohio PGA Sectional Championship. Located nearby in Concord, Quail Hollow is an 18-hole, par-72 championship course designed by Bruce Devlin who now competes on the PGA Senior Tour.

Quail Hollow, a Club Resort, is also a prime example of a phenomenal development: the weekend golf getaway. Former golf "widows" and "orphaned" children may now accompany the fairway fanatic for a fun-filled weekend at a resort that

caters to both the player and the non-golfer. Such resorts also accommodate weekend business retreats on a year-round basis.

Whatever the season, Quail Hollow has such recreational opportunities as tennis, swimming, jogging, a health spa and cross-country skiing. Typical of such resorts, it also provides posh accommodations, dining, entertainment and a fully-equipped conference center.

All told, an estimated 300,000 Cleveland area golfers play on public links. Some of the courses are tight, challenging even the seasoned pro with water hazards and hilly terrain. Others are a bit more gentle. With so many courses from which to choose, golfers can easily find the fairways best suited to their level of skill.

For the sportive Clevelander, the city provides the best of both worlds. Opportunities for water sports

are every bit as abundant as the options for the landlubber.

Lakefront State Park comprises the separate entities of Edgewater, Gordon and Wildwood parks and the E. 55th Street Marina. This extravagant shoreline draws thousands of sun worshippers, yachtsmen, swimmers, beach combers and fishermen eager to land a prized walleye.

From the East 9th Street Pier, sightseers may watch the hustle of the largest overseas general cargo port on Lake Erie. Excursion boats provide scenic trips, both on Lake Erie and the historic Cuyahoga River. And, to the delight of boat owners, marinas are only five minutes from downtown. Small craft find safe anchorage in eight acres of the new and still-developing North Coast Harbor, an $11.3 million inner harbor lake and park. Future development will include a maritime museum, an historic shipyard, a world-class aquarium and theater.

Cleveland also is an apt location for sailing events such as the Star Class World Championship and various powerboat races. Cleveland Race Week features competitions for both sailboats and powerboats.

Members of the Flats Racing League enjoy the growing sport of sculling, dipping their oars with precision as they sweep past bistros lining the Cuyahoga River's famous entertainment district. Also in the Flats, at the Nautica complex, the Boat Club offers boating instruction and access to powerboats and sailboats ranging from 28 to 70 feet in length.

While living on Lake Erie is reason enough to hang out the Gone Fishin' sign, Cleveland anglers are also tempted by rivers stocked with salmon and trout.

The Lake offers an abundance of perch and is famous for being "The Walleye Capital of the World." The Ohio Department of Natural Resources says there are 100 fishing "hot spots" near Cleveland...in breakwaters, jetties and channels...in coves and estuaries...near points and spits...and in the Lake Erie Island region as well.

Stream fishing in the Chagrin and Rocky rivers yields coho and chinook salmon, rainbow trout, channel catfish. Smaller lakes have excellent bluegill, large and small mouth bass, crappie and some rainbow trout. There are nine fishing areas in the Metroparks alone. The same lakes, ponds and streams that provide warm weather enjoyment furnish sporting pleasure for ice fishermen when snows blanket the countryside.

In Cleveland, sports and recreation knows no bounds and no season.

Companies who wish to expand, locate or start a business in Cleveland are impressed with the Greater Cleveland Growth Association's high-tech presentation center.

The Growth Association offers financial loan packaging and management assistance counseling to all Cleveland companies.

Cleveland

Impressive

The comeback city of the eighties is poised

Business

Cleveland received much acclaim in the 1980s for its well documented turnaround. Over the course of a single decade this city wrestled itself from the grips of default and wrote an innovative script for its own dramatic success story. Today, the business climate is healthy, the real estate market is soaring, development is on a roll, the city boasts an A-bond rating and the future promises more of the same. From industrial giant to rust belt decline to a rejuvenated, restructured economic base, Cleveland has come full circle.

Though it was hard to remember during the dark days of the seventies, Cleveland's proud past is primarily a tale of prosperity and growth. Throughout the latter half of the nineteenth century Cleveland began to assume its place as a thriving metropolitan city, home to such industrial giants as John D. Rockefeller, founder of the Standard Oil of Ohio Company and Marcus A. Hanna of the M.A. Hanna Company. With steel and heavy industry providing a solid foundation, Cleveland continued to be one of the nation's powerhouses as it entered the 1900s. It remained a productive, growing center through much of the century, benefitting from the industrial demands of the World Wars as well as the post World War II economic boom. As the market for steel declined in the '70s, so too did Cleveland's economy. Like many major northeastern cities,

Address

for even more dramatic growth in the nineties.

by Ann M. Zoller

Over the course of a single

decade this city wrestled

itself from the grips of

default and wrote an

innovative script for its own

dramatic success story.

Cleveland was slow to respond to a changing economy and fell victim to the plague of the rustbelt. The bottom fell out in 1978, as Cleveland suffered the sobering reality of default.

Seeing nowhere to go but up, the corporate and political communities formed an uncommon alliance and began to rally the economy. A series of public/private partnerships was the key to jumpstarting the upswing and ensuring confidence in continued economic support. Slowly and deliberately, the economic base in Cleveland shifted from heavy industry to a more stable mix, which relies heavily on service and health care. This newfound economic health, along with a greatly improved infrastructure, has attracted new businesses and an impressive array of developments.

Over $5-billion of development is currently in process or slated to take place. Cleveland is home to two of the nation's top five developers, Forest City Enterprises, Inc. and Jacobs, Visconsi and Jacobs Co. (JVJ). Both companies were able to concentrate efforts on their hometown by taking advantage of opportunities offered by Cleveland's impressive new business climate.

JVJ completed downtown's first upscale retail complex with The Galleria and Towers at Erieview in 1987. In addition, the company is changing the face of downtown's central Public Square with the construction of what will be the tallest building in Ohio — the 57-story Society Center and 400-room Marriott hotel. Soon to follow, usurping the tallest building honors in the process, will be the 60-story Ameritrust Center and 484-room Hyatt Regency hotel.

Forest City Enterprises, Inc. has just completed the first phase of its mammoth Tower City Center project. One of the largest mixed-use developments in the country, the Center currently includes a refurbished Terminal Tower office building; a glass-encased mall featuring three stories of shops, restaurants and downtown's only cineplex; two new office towers, the 14-story Ritz-Carlton hotel and Office Tower and the 12-story Skylight Office Tower; and downtown's only rail transit station, which recently completed a $5 million state-of-the-art renovation. Connected to Tower City Center is the Stouffer Tower City Plaza Hotel which is in the midst of its own massive $35-million renovation which will include a 362-room addition.

Other recent developments include the spectacular North

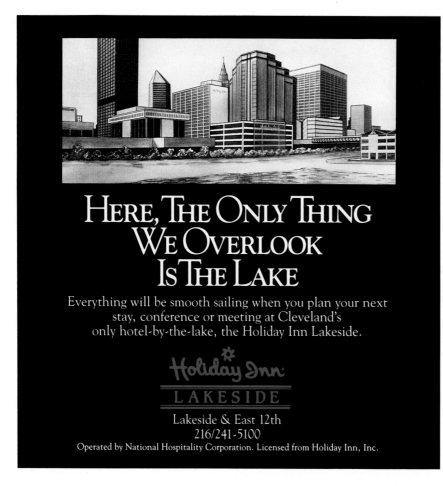

Point Tower, the 28-story Bank One Center, the striking Renaissance on Playhouse Square office tower and the Nautica entertainment complex, located in the area known as the Flats along the Cuyahoga River.

The surge in development has been complimented by an influx of new companies relocating to the area, giving Cleveland the third highest concentration of Fortune 500 industrial headquarters in the nation. Among these are Figgie International, Inc. a $1.3-billion manufacturing giant (Fortune 500); Bridgestone/Firestone, Inc. and Gould Inc., both Japanese corporations moving from Chicago; VAX Appliances, Inc. of Britain; Fanny Farmer, Inc.; and the United Church of Christ.

Enterprises already located in Cleveland, as well as those eyeing a move to the comeback city, are served by the Greater Cleveland Growth Association. It is the first metropolitan chamber of commerce in America to reach 10,000 member firms. Primary missions for the nonprofit organization include utilizing and marketing area strengths to create jobs, providing financing for growth, keeping costs down for entrepreneurs and creating jobs through high quality education programs.

In its campaign to attract new business investment, the Growth Association concentrates on industry groups that have become vital building blocks in Cleveland's economic base. These include biomedical, health services, steel, polymers, aerospace, printing, publishing and advanced manufacturing. The Association's ambassadors also stress that

Morton's of Chicago, on The Avenue at Tower City Center.

89

Cleveland's economy has achieved a remarkable balance between traditional, blue-collar manufacturing and the emerging technologies.

Mindful of significant changes in the world scenario, the Association has expanded its efforts beyond our borders. It seeks to guide Cleveland into the global market by conducting trade missions abroad, promoting reverse investment and providing export trade assistance to companies in the Cleveland area.

To encourage the creation and development of small businesses, the Growth Association — the nation's largest chamber of commerce — formed the Council of Smaller Enterprises (COSE). The biggest such organization in the United States, COSE

21 Fortune 500 industrial companies are headquartered in Greater Cleveland. Among all United States metropolitan areas, Cleveland has the 3rd largest concentration of headquarter companies.

provides small-business management training normally found only in MBA programs, but does so on a much larger scale. As a result, the local start-up pace has hit a blistering 6,000 new businesses a year.

In Cleveland's new economic base, manufacturing has shifted from 31 percent to under 23 percent of employment. Research and development, the polymer industry and some of the country's finest health care facilities are strong up-and-comers. There is the sustaining strength of well established legal and financial companies. Growth in the service industries is increasing. All of this points to a balanced and productive future for northeast Ohio.

Over $5-billion of development is currently in process or slated to take place.

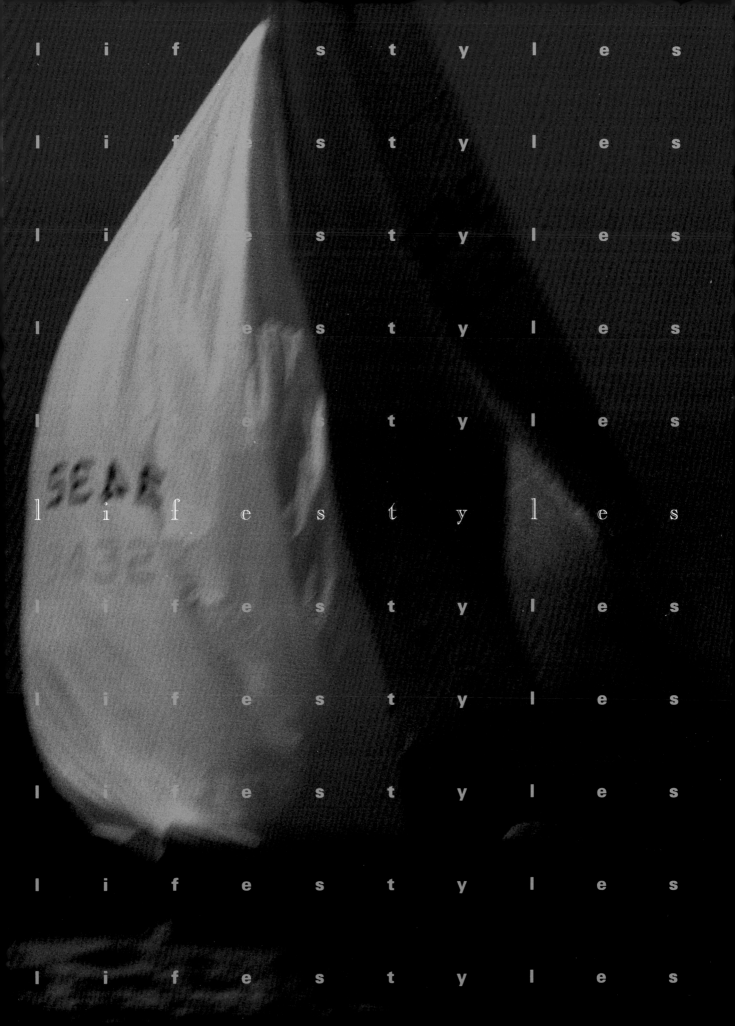

Great Living on a Great Lake

The lake, our climate, and an abundance of

fine communities provide Cleveland with an enviable

variety of lifestyle options.

Cleveland is a coastal city. This seemingly obvious statement of fact changed forever the life of the city which finally grew to understand its import. Uncovering the wonders of lakefront living over the last decade, has transformed Cleveland. We've become the North Coast. And ever since we've lived better, played harder and felt pretty good about ourselves.

As Cleveland began its much-heralded turnaround, the country began to take notice. With the national spotlight shining so intensely, Clevelanders had the opportunity to take a closer look. And we liked what we saw.

Just as we are realizing the potential offered by our beautiful waterfront environs, Clevelanders are learning to appreciate the countless other attributes we take for granted. From the glory of the four seasons, to the excellent interstate system which allows easy access throughout the city, to the abundance of impressive, affordable housing, to the enviable quality of life afforded by cultural institutions, extensive park systems and superior schools — Cleveland is very livable.

As a matter of fact, Cleveland is a great place to live. It's a place where families are raised and traditions are born. Cleveland is home.

by Ann M. Zoller

Shaker Heights

The Lake

With a prime location on Lake Erie, Clevelanders share in a unique resource. As the shallowest of the Great Lakes, Lake Erie stays warmer longer which has a direct effect on the climate of the surrounding land, the huge fish population and recreational activities. The average temperature of Lake Erie in July is 70 degrees, considerably higher than that of the other Great Lakes. This translates into a longer season for boaters, swimmers and fishermen. Likewise, the lake moderates shore temperatures, extending the growing season to 210 days per year. Surprisingly, this is comparable to that in northern Alabama. A longer spawning season for fish makes Lake Erie the "Walleye Capital of the World," which accounts in part for the one million-plus

sport fishermen on the lake.

Clearly, Cleveland's status as a waterfront community is one of its greatest assets. Remarkably, it could almost be considered a fresh, new-found attraction. In the past decade, Clevelanders have rediscovered the wonders of the water and recreational industries continue to grow, reflecting this boom.

Climate

Surprisingly, many Clevelanders will cite the climate of the city as one of the area's most appealing qualities. The splendor of the changing seasons is something most would not give up for a year of any monochromatic climate.

Winter is cold, windy and snowy. The steel gray lake seems to fight an eternal battle as white caps crash along the angry shoreline. Blankets of

snow envelop the city and turn the surrounding areas into a frosty winter wonderland. This lasts through February and occasionally into March — but gradually cold lake breezes begin to warm, bringing the irresistible delight of spring. And, absolutely nothing feels as wonderful as the first sunny, 70 degree day in Cleveland. The impact is immediate as a panorama of aromatic blossoms testify to the reawakening of the "Forest City." Greenery suddenly dominates the cityscape and hundreds of gardens seem to burst into spontaneous fits of color.

Next is summer. Summers are bright. And, Cleveland celebrates summer. Barbecues, picnics, boating and a countless menu of summer festivals make for endless excuses to savor the gifts of the great out-

doors. Although the weather can get hot, Cleveland has fewer 90 degree plus days than most other northern cities and more clear skies in June, July and August than many other parts of the country. Eventually the days grow shorter and the unmistakable feel of autumn is in the air.

Autumn in Cleveland may well be the loveliest time of the year. The spectacular kaleidoscope of changing leaves paints a breathtaking landscape throughout the city. The lush, golden days of Indian summer soothes the transition to crisp breezes of fall before another spirited winter enters.

The constant changing of the seasons keeps the city interesting and the senses alert. Life flows in a natural yet distinct calendar. Seasonal rituals become traditions which enrich lives and become ingrained into memory, ultimately defining life in Cleveland.

Communities

Cleveland offers an abundance of beautiful neighborhoods and residential communities. Lavish tudor estates, breathtaking lakefront vistas and quaintly detailed century homes are just a few of the options available in Cleveland's vast housing market. A growing string of suburbs encircles the city, most of which are within twenty miles of downtown via a well-developed freeway system. The average commute in Cleveland is only 23 minutes, which is truly an enviable benefit for a metropolitan city of Cleveland's size.

Historic Neighborhoods

Ohio City, located just west of downtown Cleveland, is one of Cleveland's oldest neighborhoods. Charming Victorian-era homes, some with two-foot-thick stone walls, are nestled among trendy neighborhood taverns and eateries in storybook fashion. Neatly tended rows of tulips peek from behind picket fences along brick lanes. Restoration of the area was spearheaded by a visionary group of urban pioneers about twenty years ago and continues today with ongoing renovation programs.
Tremont is the latest foray of the trendsetting artistic crowd. Elegantly crafted homes are available at bargain prices for those interested in renovating.
The Historic Warehouse District offers stylish loft apartments in what was Cleveland's original downtown. Located within blocks of Pub-lic Square, the Historic Warehouse District boasts some of the most beautiful architecture in the city. The area will continue to grow as more buildings are slated for renovation.
Clifton-Lake is located on Cleveland's far west side, just bordering the suburb of Lakewood. During the "Industrial Revolution" of the 1880s, members of Cleveland's elite bought huge estates on these quiet, wooded streets and built impressive homes along the lake. Many architectural styles are represented from Spanish Revival to classic ivy-covered Tudor.
Slavic Village still embraces the roots of its Eastern European heritage. Polish immigrants first arrived in the 1870s and the neighborhood

flourished due to its proximity to the steel mills. Solid older homes and "Old World" specialty shops maintain the strong neighborhood ties of this community.

Eastern Suburbs

Cleveland Heights is a sophisticated city with a multitude of housing alternatives — from the luxurious to the comfortably affordable. Spacious apartments; new condominiums; long, low ranches; contemporary split-levels; gracious colonials stately Tudors and magnificent mansions are all part of this diverse suburban community. Residents of the city enjoy a cosmopolitan feel which distinguishes Cleveland Heights from many other areas in Cleveland. Proximity to universities, hospitals, museums and other cultural attractions gives a unique urban atmosphere amidst the conveniences of a well-heeled suburb. A commitment to quality recreational facilities and programs provides yet another bonus with over 135 acres of park land available for public access. The Cleveland Heights-University Heights public school system is one of the highest rated systems in Ohio. Specially designed programs from foreign language to advanced placement help students achieve an academic edge. In addition, the city's private schools have achieved national recognition for their excellence in education. The Cleveland Heights library system is the largest system in Cuyahoga County. The city also boasts eight neighborhood shopping areas, specialty shops and fine dining — making

Cleveland Heights one of the most active, thriving communities in Cleveland. For further information, contact the Cleveland Heights Housing Service, 291-5959.

Shaker Heights is one of Cleveland's most distinctive communities. This sophisticated suburb remains among the nation's finest with superior schools, outstanding city services and magnificent homes. A planned community, with homes ranging from $60,000 – $600,000, Shaker Heights' enduring commitment to quality is ever-present. Exquisite Tudor estates featuring timeless craftsmanship and intricate detail are a testament to the tradition of excellence found in Shaker Heights. Meeting those same high stan-

dards are the area's fine Georgian and Colonial homes, two-family rentals, apartments and condominiums. The natural beauty of the area's lush green lands and the sparkling Shaker Lakes leaves an imprint of the country in the heart of this bustling city. Excellence in education is a community-wide commitment as residents take pride in their nationally recognized school system. Leisure activities are plentiful and the club-like setting of Thornton Park offers swimming, tennis and year-round ice skating. The proximity to downtown is an important advantage for the well-educated and accomplished residents of this community and is accentuated by the rapid transit, which transports com-

muters both downtown and to the airport. Shaker Heights is comprised of people who share common values — the importance of family, home and community—and the lifestyle of this vital, thriving city reflects these priorities. Shaker Heights offers an active relocation program for those interested in moving to the area. City staff members offer personalized tours of the city, schools and recreation facilities free of charge and work with realtors to meet individual needs. For information, contact the Shaker Heights Community Services Department, 491-1330.

Beachwood is one of Cleveland's wealthiest suburbs and one of its finest. Beautiful contemporary homes, exclusive retail centers, recreational amenities and an excellent school system make this suburb a superior choice.

Chagrin Falls has successfully captured the feel of an authentic New England town. Lovely century homes, quaint shops and the cascading falls for which the community is named create a picture-perfect small town setting.

Bratenahl occupies just one square mile on the shores of Lake Erie just east of downtown Cleveland. This luxurious hideaway features some of the most gorgeous estates in the country, as well as lavish condominiums and apartments. Newport, a new lakefront community with a member-owned private club and a 96-foot boat basin, offers yet another gracious option in this exclusive community.

Kopf Builders
Cleveland's Relocation Specialist

nterior design by Nancy Deeks Buffington.

Le Marchand, the crown jewel of many Kopf homes and condominiums available for immediate occupancy.

As Cleveland's largest* residential home builder, Kopf Builders is the first choice of companies relocating professionals to Cleveland, Ohio. We currently offer 11 new home and condominium communities in Avon Lake and Westlake — the two most desirable communities in western Cleveland.

Kopf Builders, with over twenty-five years of building excellence, is your logical relocation choice. Telephone 216/871-8234 or 1-800-242-8913.

Award Winning — Nationally Recognized

Professional Builder magazine 1989 Top 400 ranking

Pepper Pike is an ideal community for families. Large two-story homes sit on ample wooded lots in a serene suburban environment. An excellent school system, recreational facilities and proximity to the Metro Parks make Pepper Pike one of Cleveland's most desirable locations. **Solon** is located on the far southeastern arm of the city and is one of the fastest growing areas in the region. A wide selection of better living options are offered within this rural city, which is conveniently located off the interstate and in easy distance of many shopping centers. Residents may opt for one of the new neighborhood developments or the peaceful feel of the country along quaint lanes with abundant land and private ponds.

Western Suburbs

Lakewood boasts an extensive range of housing options from its "Gold Coast" lakefront apartments and condominiums to its tree-lined streets of duplex century homes. The excellent services, fine school system, proximity to downtown and neighborly feel of this community make Lakewood an attractive choice for many families.

Rocky River is another charming suburban retreat along the lake. Classic, understated homes line comfortable wooded streets in this traditional suburban community. Residents enjoy the convenience of nearby Westgate Mall and the upscale flair of Beachcliff Mall located in the town's center.

Bay Village is a small, picturesque community tucked neatly at the westernmost edge of the county. Huntington Beach and the Lake Erie Nature and Science Center are just two of the many attractions which offer activities for families and guests. Residents live in traditional Cape Cod and Colonial homes, as well as impressive contemporary homes, which sit on freshly manicured lawns along beautifully tended streets. Superior schools and services and a dedication to family make Bay Village one of Cleveland's best offerings.

Westlake is a comfortable upper-middle class suburb which continues to develop at a rapid pace. Many large new developments featuring both classic Georgian and Cape Cod architecture have sprung up in recent years with many more slated for the future. **Parma** is the most heavily populated suburb in Cleveland. Neatly kept, affordable housing, a wide array of shopping malls and several parks and a unique ethnic flair make Parma very livable.

Brecksville is another rapidly growing suburb. A popular choice for professionals due to its handsomely wooded lots, Brecksville is a town built to attract families.

Strongsville is the largest suburban community in Cuyahoga County. A tremendous growth spurt between 1970 – 1980 made it one of the fastest growing urban areas in the state. And growth continues in this ideal regional setting where the ambience of the country is intertwined with the modern efficiency of the most contemporary new developments. A commitment to achieving a healthy balance between the rambling park lands and running rivers and the increasing residential population will continue to attract new families to Strongsville.

The average Clevelander travels 23 minutes to work each day.

99

When
it's time
to alight...

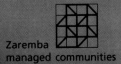

beauty all around you

Landscaping adds a special sparkle to life. Attractive plants, exciting walkways and unique wood structures bring a new dimension of beauty to your property.

Landscape architecture by Yardmaster is a process that will delight you. Our craftsmen can create your outdoor masterpiece for instant appeal.

- **Landscape architecture**
- **Planting and construction**
- **Landscape maintenance program**
- **Tree service**

YARDMASTER INC.
LANDSCAPE ARCHITECTS & CONTRACTORS
Serving all of Northeast Ohio
Phone: 951-5295